Michael,

Eph 2:8-10

7
DEADLY THOUGHTS

7
DEADLY THOUGHTS

Conquer the Thoughts that Limit Your Life

Travis H. Hall

XULON PRESS

Xulon Press
2301 Lucien Way #415
Maitland, FL 32751
407.339.4217
www.xulonpress.com

COVER DESIGN: Dianna Rivera
INTERIOR DESIGN: Michelle Cline
EDITORS: Vincent M. Newfield. Judy Godwin.

Paperback ISBN-13: 9781662806568
Ebook ISBN-13: 9781662806575

ENDORSEMENTS

My friend Travis reminds us that the battle we are engaged in is not between God and Satan, good and evil, but between our two ears—our mind! Offering practical, powerful, biblical solutions to eliminating toxic mindsets and living the abundant life you're created for, this book will become a manual for living victoriously.

—Phil Munsey
Chairman of Champions Network of Churches with Joel Osteen and Lakewood Church

Our greatest battle is fought in the internal spaces of our hearts and minds. If we are ever to win on these battlegrounds, we'd better start learning the strategies that will inevitably bring victory! Travis Hall's book, *Seven Deadly Thoughts*, identifies where we've allowed detrimental thinking to overtake our daily lives and gives practical handles to thrive with a victorious, renewed mind!

—Ben Dailey
Lead Pastor of Calvary Church, Irving, TX

In 1983, clinical psychologist M. Scott Peck introduced the Christian world to the *People of the Lie*. Travis Hall has renewed such a warning, but from the heart of a pastor who is in the trenches with real people each day. Practical, direct, and incisive, every Christian needs this book to challenge and replace the lies that we have believed.

—Dr. Josh Rice
Dean of the School of Ministry, Richmont Graduate University

My friend Travis Hall is a leader who leads with excellence and passion. Travis has anointing that changes lives and shifts atmospheres. In his new book *Seven Deadly Thoughts*, you will discover practical, biblically-based principles that will bring freedom and lead you to a greater season of promise and purpose.

—Tony Stewart
Senior Pastor, Citylife Church, Tampa, Florida

A stronghold has been defined as "a house made of thoughts." The truths in this book will enable believers to detect the lies of the enemy and to discover thoughts that are not in alignment with the truth of God's Word. When put into practice, these truths will become a powerful weapon to destroy the thoughts that are designed to prevent them from fulfilling God's plan and purpose for their life. Your house—your world—is about to change! Get ready to think, speak, and live differently; to be the person you were created to be.

—Bishop Mitch Corder
Director of Church Health and Revitalization Cleveland, TN

Through the years I have observed the people who make the greatest impact and achieve their God-given purpose have one thing in common...they've learned to master their minds. That is the reason you need to read and reread *Seven Deadly Thoughts*. Chapter after chapter, Pastor Travis shines a light on common lies we often believe while revealing timeless truths that reprogram our thinking for success and significance.

—Joe Dobbins
Lead Pastor of Twin Rivers Church, St. Louis, MO

Travis Hall has crafted a brilliant masterpiece of writing, integrating biblical teaching and real-life application in this authentic, transparent, and impactful book. Every person reading *Seven Deadly Thoughts* will be empowered by the practical guidance and life-changing inspiration offered in the wealth of each chapter.

—Dr. Sean S. O'Neal
Administrative Bishop for the Church of God, California

Pastor Travis Hall is one of the more positively influential people that I know. In his new book, *Seven Deadly Thoughts*, he writes to readers directly from his heart. The book cuts to the core of the self-perception problems that plague so many of us. We are bombarded with negative input: human life doesn't matter, people are expendable, survival is the best we can hope for... As long as our self-concept is toxic, our lives will be poisoned. I highly advise all leaders to read this work and to teach it to their teams. Bishop Hall provides a valuable resource, one that may bring into reality the possibility of a life-altering transformation!

—Rick Whitter
Administrative Bishop, Illinois Church of God

Travis Hall is an anointed and effective leader who has captured the strategy of the enemy to destroy God's purpose in our lives and given us a road map to be victorious and not victims. The principles shared from his own experiences will build your faith and sharpen your mind to battle the enemy.

—Bishop Tom Madden
Administrative Bishop, North Georgia Church of God

You may have heard it said, "We've never done it that way before," as the seven words of a dying church. *Seven Deadly Thoughts* is based on the concept that these phrases, quotes, and negativity are things that can grow in the mind of an individual. They can keep you from your future and your destiny, and even cause you to deny your promise from the Father. *Seven Deadly Thoughts* not only exposes these things but provides solutions for you to learn how to overcome these thoughts and to change your mind. Romans 12 challenges us to renew our mind. Change your mind. Transform your mind. This book is a must read to be on the shelf in every believer's library. Be encouraged today as you incorporate the mind of Christ into your everyday living and overcome these seven deadly thoughts.

—Dr. Tim Hill
General Overseer, The Church of God

For Tina:
Your love wraps courage
around my heart.

CONTENTS

Chapter 1

BELIEVING A LIE IS THE TRUTH

I see another law at work in me, waging war
against the law of my mind and making me a prisoner...
~Romans 7:23 (NIV)

"Change your thoughts and you change your world."

~Norman Vincent Peale[1]

It would be a mistake to assume that the presence of a stronghold in your life is always obvious, because it isn't. One of the most surprising realities of deadly thinking is that you can be held captive by one for years and be totally unaware. Strongholds typically arrive unannounced. They creep in quietly and develop in your thought life with the purpose of poisoning your perspective. And strongholds come in all shapes and sizes. There are religious strongholds, relational strongholds, fear-based strongholds, and strongholds that keep you from enjoying the abundant life that Jesus died and rose again for you to experience. The enemy is so subtle that you often don't even sense his activity until the damage has already been done, and you are left to pick up the pieces of your life after years of making destructive decisions.

Somewhere in your life, God has called you to lead. Whether it is at home, in a board room, at church, or in school, you were created to impact the world around you. According to Ephesians

2:10, there are "good works" you've been put on earth to accomplish. The enemy is very much aware of that, so he's made it his mission to establish destructive thought patterns in your mind that will sabotage your success and choke out your ability to build the life that God has created you to build. The enemy wants to influence your thinking and poison your perception so you'll see yourself as something less than how God sees you.

This battle for our thoughts is real, and we're not the first ones to experience it. While teaching the Corinthian church a lesson on winning spiritual battles, the apostle Paul explained that if we're ever going to win the war against deadly thinking, we must learn how to tear down the **strongholds** that have been established in our minds. He wrote:

> "For the weapons of our warfare are not carnal but mighty in God for pulling down strongholds, casting down arguments and every high thing that exalts itself against the knowledge of God, bringing every thought into captivity to the obedience of Christ."

> **—2 Corinthians 10:4-5 (NKJV)**

In her book *Battlefield of the Mind*, Joyce Meyer describes a stronghold this way:

> "A stronghold is an area in which we are held in bondage, [it's] any part of our lives in which Satan imprisons us. He does this by causing us to think a certain way—a way that is based on lies we have been told."[2]

Perhaps the best definition of a *stronghold* is simply: *believing that a lie is the truth*.

It Begins at the Earliest Age

The enemy doesn't appear to waste any time in his attempts to inflict pain for the sake of establishing strongholds that will last a lifetime. "The younger the better" appears to be his motto when it comes to launching his attack. According to Revelation 12:4, Satan begins his work when we are children.

> "...And the dragon stood before the woman who was about to give birth, so that when she gave birth he might devour her child."

> **Revelation 12:4 (NASB)**

While this is a clear reference to the birth of Jesus and the enemy's plan to eliminate Him before He could fulfill His purpose, it also reveals the strategy of the enemy. Before you were born, your adversary, the devil, started to strategize ways he could inflict deep wounds in your soul—wounds through which he could traffic destructive thoughts–strongholds he could set in place that would eventually devour your destiny and keep you from enjoying the abundant life and fulfilling your own God-given purpose.

For you, maybe those wounds came through the hurtful words of a parent who told you things like, "You're such a loser! You never finish anything you start," or, "You'll never amount to anything! I don't even know why you were born." Maybe you were abused, rejected, neglected, or abandoned, and you know that the majority of the decisions you make today are somehow connected to the painful places of yesterday.

Perhaps it wasn't the destructive words of someone you loved that hurt you, but rather their silence and lack of affirmation that left you wounded. Maybe as a result you thought you weren't lovable and ended up looking for love in all the wrong places. Or maybe you've spent years trying to prove your self-worth by burying yourself in your work to the point of neglecting the important people in your life. Maybe you've tried to numb all that pain through toxic relationships, sexual encounters, or drugs and alcohol, only leaving your heart feeling even more empty than before, reinforcing the destructive mindset of *I'm not enough, and I'll never be enough.*

The Poison of Pain

Like scar tissue forming after an injury, strongholds often develop subtly in our lives after we've been wounded. As a result, when life gets hard, we're tempted to retreat from God and His promises in order to avoid the possibility of being hurt again, or having to deal with more disappointment down the road. We convince ourselves that the walls we've built around our heart are there to protect us, but instead they imprison us. We become slaves to fear rather than ambassadors of faith.

Building these internal walls and retreating when things get hard always starts in our mind before it shows up in our life. Quitting, after all, is a mindset—a dangerous stronghold that serves to poison our divine purpose. Pastors and church leaders walk away emotionally from ministry long before they ever submit their resignation. Likewise, husbands and wives walk away from their marriages in their hearts way before they ever step foot in an attorney's office to file for a divorce.

A stronghold will rob you of...

- The peace that God promised you.
- The joy that God promised you.
- The abundant life God's Word says is yours.

The pain created by strongholds will cause you to build relationships with all the wrong people while pushing away all the right ones. Sometimes you can tell when a stronghold is present by the way you talk. If you often find yourself speaking in the language of the past—talking about what *could have been, should have been,* or *might have been*—it is a good indicator that a stronghold of wrong thinking is actively at work.

4

One of the Enemy's Most Enticing Lies

A stronghold will cause a person to believe they're absolutely right when they're positively wrong. According to the apostle Paul in 2 Corinthians 10:5, one of Satan's purposes for establishing strongholds in our minds is to introduce "speculations" or "thoughts" that exalt themselves against the knowledge of God. In other words, the enemy works to convince us that somehow we know more (or better) than God does.

Now, I understand that initially this sounds ridiculous. After all, who in the world would actually claim to know more than God, right? However, the reality is this sort of attack is launched against our thought life every day. Unfortunately, we often don't recognize it as a spiritual attack when it is happening, so we wind up falling for it more than we realize.

For example, have you ever been reading the Bible when suddenly it felt like a verse or passage jumped off the page? In that moment, you knew that what you just read was nothing less than God speaking directly to you, and it was exactly what you needed to hear. You were both excited and overwhelmed by His favor and goodness!

Or maybe you unexpectedly received an encouraging word through your pastor, a friend, or a coworker about something going on in your life that they knew nothing about. There was no way they could have been aware of your life circumstances. Yet their message was so spot-on that you had no doubt God was speaking directly to you through them. You then walked away from that divine encounter supernaturally energized and ready to take on the world!

Then suddenly something tragic happened. You found yourself in the midst of a trial or setback, and within 24 hours of hearing from God, you began to "lean on your own understanding." You began focusing on all of the reasons why those promises the Lord just gave you could never come to pass in your life. You started focusing on your circumstances and limitations. You began thinking thoughts like, *I'm too old, I'm too young, I'm too broke, I'm too hurt, I'm in too deep of a mess, I've made way too many mistakes,* or *It's too late."*

Before you knew it, you accepted one or more of these lies as the truth and reasoned away all of the promises of God. Without even realizing it, you became the victim of a *stronghold,* and your life was put on hold. You, like many others, believed the lie that you knew more than your Maker. And all of this began when you accepted (or took ownership of) a "thought" or "speculation" that exalted itself against the knowledge of God.

Experiencing the Transformed Life

Are you catching a glimpse of what the enemy has been up to in your life? Are you beginning to see why it is so vital that we learn how to "take wrong thoughts captive to the obedience of Christ"? By learning to retrain your brain to recognize and reject the lies of the enemy, you can get your life out of the ditch and see God's wonderful promises fulfilled.

As a pastor, I have seen countless people full of incredible potential held captive by strongholds of wrong thinking, and it breaks my heart. Their potential is being held captive by low thoughts about themselves and their God. The truth is, you can be born again, forgiven of all your sins and have your name written down in what the Bible calls the Book of Life, yet still be dealing with deadly thinking. Look at the people of Israel. They had just been miraculously set free from over 400 years of bondage and slavery. However, when things got tough on their journey to the Promised Land, their first instinct was to go back to their bondage.

> "So they said to one another, 'Let us appoint a leader and return to Egypt.'"

> **Numbers 14:4 (NASB)**

Why did God's chosen people want to return to Egypt, the place of their bondage and slavery? Because while they were free in body, they were still held captive in their minds. No matter

6

how hard we try to prop ourselves up with new and improved behavior, our lives will always default back to the way we think. God's people were technically free, but they were still thinking like slaves.

Far too many believers are trying to live a new life without a renewed mind, and it's just not possible. In Romans 12:2 the apostle Paul teaches us that in order to experience a transformed life, we must first undergo the process of renewing our minds. Until we experience a transformed mind, we'll never experience a transformed life. As King Solomon wrote in Proverbs 23:7 (KJV), as a man "...thinketh in his heart, so is he..."

The good news? Jesus is stronger than every stronghold! He didn't die on the cross and rise from the dead just so you could remain a captive to deadly thinking. On the contrary, He redeemed you to become a new creation, fulfill your God-given purpose, live the abundant life, and advance His Kingdom. He provided you with divine authority and spiritual weapons that, when used properly, will enable you to win the war against the enemy's strategy. These are weapons of mass destruction—"mighty in God for pulling down strongholds" (2 Corinthians 10:4 NKJV). Jesus has given you power and authority to destroy every stronghold and take every ungodly thought into captivity. But first you must begin to renew your mind and be willing to confront wrong thinking.

I've discovered that you can have God's best for your life, but only if you *think* you can. While it's impossible to forecast every deadly thought that Satan will bring to your mind in his attempt to establish a stronghold, you can equip yourself with the knowledge you need to be able to identify his lies and get victory over some of the most common and destructive thoughts in his arsenal. With God's help, you can identify and demolish the kind of strongholds that tear apart families, marriages, businesses and churches. You can learn to detect and deal with thoughts that try to convince you to quit before you ever get started.

In the pages that follow, we're going to learn how to recognize and eliminate seven of the deadliest thoughts you'll encounter throughout the course of your life. If we're going to move our lives and leadership forward, these *Seven Deadly Thoughts* must be taken captive to the obedience of Christ. And by His grace, they will be!

Chapter 2

THE TRAP OF LOW THINKING

For as the heavens are higher than the earth,
so are My ways higher than your ways
and My thoughts than your thoughts.
~ Isaiah 55:9 (NASB)

"Progress is impossible without change, and those
who cannot change their minds cannot change
anything."[3]

~ George Bernard Shaw

The quality of your life and leadership will never exceed the quality of your thoughts. Your marriage, your ministry, and the amount of money you are able to earn and enjoy will always be directly linked to the quality of your thought life.

In the Old Testament book of Isaiah God declares, "...My ways are higher than your ways, and My thoughts are higher than your thoughts." Usually, this is a passage we quote when we find ourselves in the presence of real-life circumstances that are way out of our control. It becomes our catch-all verse when we don't have the answers to the myriad of "why" questions that we're faced with on this side of heaven. But to stop with this meaning alone is to miss something very significant. I think God was trying to teach us something more.

Please don't get me wrong. It brings me tremendous comfort to know that when life doesn't make sense, God always knows what He's doing. That's a truth I've had to cling to more times than I can remember. Yet I believe in this specific passage of scripture that God is revealing to us another pivotal truth: His thoughts and His actions (ways) are eternally and inseparably intertwined with each other.

Just in case you didn't catch that, let me say it one more time. *God's thoughts and actions (His ways) are inseparably intertwined with each other.*

When I read Isaiah 55:9, I don't just hear God saying, "Hey guys, don't sweat it. I know you don't understand what's going on right now, but I've got a plan...I'm working." I also hear our loving heavenly Father calling to His children, saying, "My son...My daughter, who in the world has taught you how to think such low, condemning, self-defeating thoughts? It's time to think *higher thoughts.* It's time to think more like your heavenly Father thinks!"

Now I'm not suggesting even for a moment that our finite minds would ever be able to comprehend all of the infinite thoughts of our great God. However, I do believe that we often place limits on God's activity in our lives, and these restraints can always be traced back to the way we think. Often times we unknowingly limit God by our self-defeated, low-level thought life.

So what's the key to unlocking the next level of your life and place of leadership? I can guarantee you it won't be found in getting a new promotion at work or a pay raise. You also won't discover it by earning your Master's Degree, finding the right person to spend the rest of your life with, or obtaining a new rank in ministry. While all of these things are fantastic and can indeed help you pursue and fulfill your purpose, unlocking the next level of your life and place of leadership will only be experienced when you choose to take the limits off of your stinking thinking and begin to think higher thoughts.

Low Thinking Can Be Lethal

In his book *Your Best Life Now*, Pastor Joel Osteen shares the story of a hard-working, but low-thinking man named Nick. Nick was a chronically negative railroad worker who managed to lock himself inside a refrigerated box car that was in desperate need of maintenance work, which is where things went horribly wrong. Pastor Osteen wrote:

> "Aware that he was in a refrigerated boxcar, Nick guessed that the temperature in the unit was well below freezing, maybe as low as five- or ten-degrees Fahrenheit. Nick feared the worst. He thought, *What am I going to do? If I don't get out of here, I'm going to freeze to death. There's no way I can stay in here all night.* The more he thought about his circumstances, the colder he became. With the door shut tightly, and no apparent way of escape, he sat down to await his inevitable death by freezing or suffocation, whichever came first. The next morning, when the crews came to work, they opened the boxcar and found Nick's body crumpled over in the corner. When the autopsy was completed, it revealed that Nick had indeed frozen to death. Now, here's a fascinating enigma: The investigators discovered that the refrigeration unit for the car in which Nick had been trapped was not even on! In fact, it had been out of order for some time and was not functioning at the time of the man's death. The temperature in the car that night— the night Nick froze to death—was sixty-one degrees. Nick froze to death in slightly less than normal room temperatures because he believed that he was in a freezing boxcar...He expected the worst. He saw himself as doomed with no way out. He lost the battle in his own mind."[4]

Nick's story personifies the words of King Solomon in Proverbs 23:7 (KJV): "As [a man] thinketh in his heart, so is he..." Nick *thought* he was going to freeze to death, so he did.

You can go on a diet to lose weight, but if you don't change the way you think about food, you'll only put the weight back on again. You can change jobs in order to make more money and get out of debt, but no matter how much money you make, unless you change the way you think about money, you'll only end up back in debt again.

As it turns out, low thinking affects marriages too, and in a big way. According to a report from *Psychology Today*, 50 percent of first marriages, 67 percent of second marriages, and 73 percent of third marriages all end in divorce.[5] Statistically, the more a person gets married and divorced, the more likely they are to get divorced again. Now maybe it's just me, but doesn't it seem like the more you do something, the better you should get at it? Yet according to these numbers, by the time someone gets to their third marriage, they only have a 27 percent chance of making it last. The reason for this diminishing rate of marital success is that people keep going into a new marriage with the same old mindset. This is the danger of thinking low thoughts.

- Some people *think* they'll never accomplish anything great in their lives, and so they don't.
- Some people constantly *think* that their marriage will never make it, and so it doesn't.
- Some people waste years of their lives *thinking* they'll never be happy, healthy, healed, or whole, and so they aren't.

In each of these situations, nothing good happens. Not because it can't, but because they don't *think* that it can. This is the dangerous reality of low thinking. It can be lethal.

Created in His Image

You and I are created by God in His very image (see Genesis 1:27). Therefore, since His thoughts can't be separated from His ways, that means our ways (actions and attitudes) are inseparably and eternally connected to our thoughts as well! John Maxwell said it this way: "That which holds our attention determines our actions. We are where we are and what we are because of the dominating thoughts that occupy our minds."[6]

Just like your Creator, you cannot separate the way you *think* from the way you *act*. If you're constantly thinking negative thoughts, then you'll constantly produce a negative life. You'll always be waiting and believing for the worst possible scenario, and you'll find yourself defeated before the fight even begins. If you continually criticize yourself internally with thoughts like, *I'll never be a good leader, I'll never be good with money, I'll never get my temper under control*, or *I'll never be physically fit*, then you'll likely spend the rest of your life living out the *low* actions and attitudes required to fulfill those low, negative thoughts. Why? Because people who don't think much of themselves won't do much with themselves.

Seeing from the Outside In

When God changes us, He works from the *inside out*—He *thinks* about and *sees* us transformed from within first, and *then* without. Unfortunately, we tend to *think* and see things just the opposite—from the outside in. This was the way in which the Pharisees thought, always focusing on outward appearances and superficial traditions that had no eternal value. Jesus addressed this issue of deadly thinking at its core 2,000 years ago. In Matthew 23:26 (NLT) He told the Pharisees, and us:

> "...First wash the *inside* of the cup, ...and then the outside will become clean, too."

The Pharisees often get a bad rap as it pertains to spiritual leadership, and in most cases rightfully so. However, the truth is that like the Pharisees, we also often suffer from outside-in thinking. We try to change our actions without inviting Jesus to help us change the way we think, and it just doesn't work. The apostle Paul made it clear that the only way our lives are transformed is by "...the renewing of your mind" (Romans 12:2 NIV). How does this renewing of the mind take place? It's primarily a work of the Holy Spirit within you. When he wrote to the church in Ephesus in Ephesians 4:23-24 (NLT), Paul said, "...let the Spirit renew your thoughts and attitudes. Put on your new nature, created to be like God—truly righteous and holy." The moment you place your faith in Jesus, the Spirit begins the glorious work of renewing your mind and giving you a new life, but it works from the inside out, not the other way around. It requires us to be patient with ourselves and to trust that Jesus loves us and won't leave us just because it's taking time to see the change on the outside that's happening on the inside. He knows how long it's taking because He's the One doing the work, and in the meantime, He still loves you and refuses to leave you.

I've watched people with an outside-in mindset go on a shopping spree when they were feeling down. They think that by purchasing new clothes, gadgets, or even a new car they will somehow magically become a new person. The reality is, they're just dressing up their old low thinking. Like the Pharisees, they're only cleaning the outside of the cup rather than choosing to trust God with the most important part—the inside.

We can whiten our teeth, fix our smile, shed unwanted weight and get in shape, or finance thousands of dollars on plastic surgery. But until we change the way we think about ourselves, none of these things is going to make us truly happy. Regardless of all the exterior improvements, we're still left to face the way we think about ourselves.

Spending money on new stuff may temporarily numb the feelings of emptiness and even give you a brief boost in self-worth, but eventually the thrill of new clothes, cars, or a new relationship is going to wear off. The pain of emptiness produced by low thinking can only be relieved by choosing to think about yourself the same way God thinks about you. If you're going to effectively tear down the strongholds that limit your life and leadership, you have to be willing, with God's help, to "wash the inside of the cup" first. See yourself the way your heavenly Father sees you, and accept what Jesus did for you on the cross as being enough. Then and only then will "...the outside become clean, too."

Learning to Love Yourself

As you learn how to love yourself the way God loves you, you'll realize that you don't need a new house, car, or new clothes to like who you are. After all, you are created in the image of God, you are fearfully and wonderfully made, and in Christ, you're loved, affirmed, and accepted by your heavenly Father! Every time God looks at you, His child, He sees a reflection of Himself. The true confidence you need and the loving acceptance you crave doesn't depend on what you're wearing or anything else others see on the outside. It comes from knowing and believing what God thinks of you. The truth is, you may not even be sure what kind of stuff you really like because you've spent your entire life liking things you thought you needed to like in order to get other people to love you. If this sounds familiar, it may be time to rediscover the masterpiece of you!

You can be financially broke, but still be confident. You can be alone, but still be happy. You can be left out of the clique or overlooked at work, but when you start thinking about and seeing yourself the way that God thinks about and sees you, you'll be able to stand confidently without compromising your own unique one-of-a-kind identity. Regardless of the circumstances, you'll be able to say, "I keep my eyes always on the Lord...I will not be shaken" (Psalm 16:8 NIV).

If you think about it, every aspect of your life comes back to your ability to, as Jesus said, "...love yourself." Trying to love others without first learning how to love yourself is outside-in thinking. It's also a dysfunctional mindset that results in deeper, more lasting pain. I've watched people go from person to person, friend to friend, and even marriage to marriage trying to get from others what can only be received from God. You'll never be able to love other people correctly until you can first love yourself the way God loves you. In his book *Attitude 101*, author and leadership expert John C. Maxwell says it this way:

> "It is impossible to perform consistently in a manner inconsistent with the way we see ourselves. In other words, we usually act in direct response to our self-image. Nothing is more difficult to accomplish than changing outward actions without changing inward feelings...How we see ourselves reflects how others see us. If we like ourselves, it increases the odds that others will like us. Self-image sets the parameters for the construction of our attitudes. We act in response to how we see ourselves. We will never go beyond the boundaries that stake out our true feelings about ourselves. Those 'new territories' can be explored only when our self-image is strong enough to give us permission to go there."[7]

If you are trying to get the people around you to love you *before* you love yourself, you are in for a roller coaster ride of emotions. On one hand you want to be loved, but on the other hand you keep pushing people away. Why? Because it's hard to receive love from someone else when deep down inside you don't truly believe you deserve it. This is a vicious cycle that, without trusting in Jesus and His unconditional love, you can never win. Eventually, you'll drain the life out of your relationships because you're trying to extract something from people that they simply cannot give you. Exhausted from the struggle, those around you will ultimately jump ship. They'll often walk away from the relationship in order to save their own sense of self-worth and preserve their sanity.

The good news is there is one Person Who will never jump ship. He has promised to never leave you nor forsake you. In fact,

He is the only One Who has exactly what you need—uncondi-tional love and acceptance, and He can give you the ability to love yourself. No matter how much you initially struggle to love yourself, Jesus will never stop loving you. He has a divine ability to love people who are unable to love themselves. He offers a supernatural, out-of-this-world kind of love—a love that heals and gives life and forgiveness. His love is unconditional, trans-forming the way you see and think about yourself. He is the King and Creator of the universe Who loves you so deeply that He allowed Himself to be tortured and nailed to a cross before rising again from the dead in order to give you new life. That's the kind of love that Jesus offers you, and He's ready to teach you how to think *higher thoughts*.

What Are *Higher Thoughts?*

Now, I want to be clear here. When I say that we need to think "higher thoughts" about ourselves, I'm not talking about the kind of prideful, self-exalting thoughts that got Satan kicked out of heaven. God specifically instructs us in Romans 12:3 (NASB) that man is "...not to think more highly of himself than he ought to think..." We'll talk more about the wrong kind of "high thinking" in greater depth later on, but for now you need to know that the kind of *higher thinking* I'm talking about is not in any way connected to the self-serving thoughts that the apostle Paul was tackling in his letter to the Roman church.

The kind of *higher thoughts* that I'm talking about is the kind of thinking that enables you to "Set your mind on the things above, not on the things that are on earth" (Colossians 3:2 NASB). It is the kind of thinking that empowers you to "...lay aside the old self" by being "...renewed in the spirit of your mind" (Ephesians 4:22-23 NASB). I'm talking about giving the Creator more credit, appreciation, and praise for *you* in your thinking. You are His incredible creation!

The Bible says that God loves you so much and thinks so highly of you that He put His very own stamp on your life to make sure that everyone would know not just "who" you are, but also

"Whose" you are. According to Genesis 1:26 (NASB), "...God said, 'Let Us make man in Our image, according to Our likeness...'" By making you in His image, He put His own name on the line. In the purest way possible, He is so proud to call you His own that He, the Creator of the universe, created you in His own image.

This is just one of God's *higher thoughts* that He thinks about you. And since He thinks this about you, you should think it about you also. With confidence, you can say, "I am made in the very image of God! He loves me so much that He has placed His own DNA stamp on my life! He has great value, and on the cross He proved that He thinks I have great value too!"

God's Thoughts Toward You

What other *higher thoughts* is God thinking about you? In Jeremiah 29:11 (NKJV) the Lord says, "For I know the *thoughts* that I *think* toward you, says the Lord, *thoughts* of peace and not of evil, to give you a future and a hope." What an encouraging truth! God *has been*, *is now*, and *will be for eternity* thinking precious and innumerable thoughts toward you—thoughts to give you peace, hope, and a future.

In Psalm 139:17-18 (NASB) David, under the inspiration of the Holy Spirit, wrote concerning God's thoughts toward us. He said, "How precious also are Your thoughts to me, O God! How vast is the sum of them! If I should count them, they would outnumber the sand."

Through the prophet Jeremiah, the Lord also makes this declaration: "Before I formed you in the womb I knew [and] approved of you [as My chosen instrument]..." (Jeremiah 1:5 AMPC).

Do you realize the weight of what you just read? Do you realize the power that's packed into these eternal and unchangeable truths? When you take what we've learned so far—that God's thoughts and His ways are inseparably connected to one another—and then add these three scriptures, it becomes the one-two punch that has the power to KO every kind of low self-condemning thought you've ever struggled with, or ever will struggle with, in your entire life! Look at these facts:

- Before you were formed in your mother's womb, the Lord approved of you.
- God has been, is now, and will be for eternity thinking precious and innumerable thoughts toward you—thoughts to give you peace, hope, and a future.
- God's thoughts are inseparably connected to actions.

BOOM! The fact that God is **thinking** about you means that God is also **taking actions** on your behalf! You may not be able to see it or feel it right now, but even as you're reading this, God is working behind the scenes, bringing your life into divine alignment.

God's thoughts toward you = God's actions toward you

God's THOUGHTS of "peace, hope, and a future" for you are "precious and innumerable." At the same time, His ACTIONS toward you are also "precious and innumerable." Those actions (aka blessings and promises) will all result in "peace, hope, and a blessed future!" The Bible reveals that, "...the **eyes** of the Lord run **to and fro** throughout the whole earth, **to** show Himself strong on behalf of *those* whose heart *is* loyal **to** Him" (2 Chronicles 16:9 NKJV).

How many blessings are coming your way? According to Psalm 139:18, you should expect them to "outnumber the sand" on the seashore. That alone is enough to make you stop right now and thank Him—not only for what He's done, but also for what He's going to do in the days ahead.

An Overlooked Form of Worship

There is one thing that is very clear about David in the Bible: he knew "who" he was. Yes, he was the giant killer. Yes, he was king of Israel. However, there was more to his awareness, something deeper that energized him. David knew "who" he was because he knew "Whose" he was. In Psalm 139:14 he boldly and unapologetically declared:

> "I will give thanks to You, for **I am** fearfully and wonderfully made; **Wonderful are Your works**, And my soul knows it very well."

—Psalm 139:14 (NASB)

The reason David could slay his giants and kill "tens of thousands" of his enemies was not because he had better equipment than the other soldiers or because he had better opportunities. David simply chose to think *higher thoughts* than the other men. His reasoning was simple: He knew his God was great, and so by default he knew God's workmanship (himself) was second to none. David knew he was created in the image of God and reflected God's greatness—not because he was perfect, but because of God's perfection living in him through His image. The same thing is true for you and me.

The New Living Translation renders the second half of David's words in Psalm 139:14 this way: "...Your workmanship is marvelous— how well I know it." Do you realize who David is speaking about here? It's himself. He is not being arrogant or cocky. This, ladies and gentlemen, is a Psalm. In other words, this is PRAISE to God! David is worshiping God by acknowledging God's workmanship.

If you spend all of your time thinking little of yourself, then you're subconsciously training yourself to think little of God. In fact, maybe the reason so many people struggle to *genuinely* worship God is because they have so many low thoughts about themselves, His creation.

You knowing *who* you are, and more importantly *Whose* you are, releases you to truly worship God and slay your giants just as David did. Understanding that your existence is evidence of God's greatness is vital! When you choose to think higher thoughts about you, His creation, you think higher thoughts about your

Creator. These aren't prideful thoughts. They're just "right" thoughts recorded as *worship* in the Scripture.

Don't Listen to the Devil

Satan does not want you to worship Jesus. That's why he works so hard to muzzle you, and all of God's people, by getting you to think very lowly of yourself and, consequently, lowly of God. Satan is so afraid of your discovering the quality of your own workmanship that the moment you start to believe you are who God says you are, he leans over and whispers thoughts of shame and religious condemnation.

How can you think for one minute that you are good, he mutters. *You're just being prideful, thinking more highly of yourself than you should. Remember all those mistakes you made in your life?*

'Sound familiar? I always say that if Satan can't puff you up in pride, he'll pull you down in condemnation. He will work very hard to get you to think less and less of yourself and to believe that because of the mistakes you've made, you've disqualified yourself for everything good that the Father has for you. But it's not about the mistakes you've made; it's about the sacrifice Jesus made for you on the cross; and because of the cross, you're qualified for everything good that your heavenly Father has for you. The only time the enemy wants you to speak up is when you're agreeing with the way he thinks about you rather than the way God thinks about you. Maybe getting you to think so little of yourself is nothing more than his strategy to keep you a slave to all of your personal giants. After all, Satan knows that you will lose 100 percent of the battles that you refuse to fight. Therefore, his best strategy is to keep you thinking you can never win.

But remember, *Satan is a liar!*

Now you might say, "But, I was actually taught to think lowly of myself for as long as I can remember," and I understand. You may have had low thinking engrained in you for so long that a stronghold has been established in your mind, causing you to have a really hard time accepting that God wants you to think more highly of yourself. This is a super-common reality for many. Therefore, to help you grab hold of this, I want to put it to you another way.

How can you claim to think so highly of God and then turn around and think so little of yourself? What does that say about the God Who created you? What does that say *to* the God Who created you? If God thinks so highly of you that He created you in His image, then who are we to argue with the supreme value of God's workmanship? Perhaps an even better question is, "Why is Satan so afraid of your knowing who you are?" In his book *Altar Ego*, Pastor and bestselling author Craig Groeschel said it this way:

> "If you follow Christ, then you have access to his power. You might not think of yourself as extraordinary, but the fact is, there's no such thing as an ordinary Christian. You are a Spirit-filled overcomer."[8]

Charting a New Course

As we come to the end of this chapter, take a few moments to take an inventory of your "low places." In what areas of your life do you feel the most frustrated and can't seem to make any lasting progress? Is it in your relationship with God, your marriage, or your relationship with your kids? Is it in your finances— that no matter what you do, you just can't seem to get ahead? Maybe you have had a hard time losing weight and staying in shape beyond the first two months of a new year. Or worst of all, maybe you're convinced that God is angry with you, that He would never accept you or that He's perpetually disappointed with you, and so you can never just enjoy your relationship with

Jesus and the abundant life He's promised. Whatever your *low places* may be, you need to understand that the low places in your life are directly connected to the *low places* in your mind.

Now you might be saying to yourself, *Hold on a minute! If God's thoughts to bless me outnumber the sand on the sea shore, then where are all of those "vast" and "precious" blessings? I mean, I could use a few of those right about now, but I don't see anything anywhere!* That's a great question. If you will allow me, I'd like to answer it with another question: Are all of the low thoughts you're thinking about yourself keeping you from experiencing all of the "high" thoughts that God is thinking toward you?

Generally speaking, your life can't go where your mind hasn't already been. The permission that you need to take your life to a higher level doesn't begin with making other people "think" differently about you. It begins with YOU thinking differently about you. Don't waste any more time trying to change other people's opinions of you. True freedom will come as you change your own opinion of yourself and begin to think *higher thoughts* like your Creator thinks.

It's time to stop all the negative self-talk and start believing what the Word of God says about you! Begin to see yourself and think about yourself the way that God does. Say, "God loves me, yes *me*! I am fearfully and wonderfully made in the very image of God Himself! God is thinking good thoughts about me and toward me—thoughts of peace, hope, and a good future. He is actively working to bring about these good things right now. I praise You and thank You, God, for exposing and annihilating every trace of low thinking in my life!"

Chapter 3

A POISONED PERCEPTION

*The lamp of the body is the eye. If therefore your eye is good,
your whole body will be full of light. But if your eye is bad,
your whole body will be full of darkness...*
~ Matthew 6:22-23 (NKJV)

"Perception is reality."

~ Unknown

Perception is powerful. Webster defines *perception* as "the ability to see, hear, or become aware of something through the senses." It's basically a *mental impression* that's built on our past experiences, but it continues to evolve every single day of our lives as we encounter new experiences and information. Essentially, perception serves as a sort of *filter* through which we view the world around us. Whether it is good or bad, everything we see and hear has to pass through this all important filter of our own personal perception.

This is where things can get dangerous, because if we're not equipped to protect our perception against deadly thinking, we can unknowingly allow contaminated thoughts to become strongholds in our minds, poisoning our perception and darkening the lens through which we view the world. Let me explain.

Has someone ever told you something negative about someone else that changed your ability to see that person the same way, only to find out later that the information you received was inaccurate? Yet, even though you learned the knowledge you'd been given was incorrect, the feelings and thoughts you developed as a result of that gossip were still present every time you saw that person. That is, you had a very hard time getting past that erroneous information. The mental impression you constructed attached itself to your emotions and seemed impossible to shake off. That's the danger of a poisoned perception. The enemy's objective is to attack and poison your perception of yourself and others. If Satan can alter the way you see yourself and others, he can place a stumbling block between you and your purpose.

Poison Control

When I was in the second grade, a man from the Poison Control department came into our classroom to talk to us about the potential dangers of common chemicals. Once a year he'd come and point out some of the everyday household items that kids should never handle—and more importantly, never swallow. Every time he came to our school, he would send us home with a handful of these round, bright green "yuck" stickers that we were supposed to give to our parents so they could stick them on all of the household items that could be deadly if consumed. Every time I opened up the cupboard just below our kitchen sink and saw those green stickers on a bottle of bleach or liquid Drano, it reminded me of the talk we heard from that guy and the dangers of swallowing poison. Apparently, his talks worked because I managed to get through life without eating any laundry soap or using the 409 as breath freshener.

Unfortunately, while they taught us about the dangers of drinking poison and the effects it would have on our bodies, no one ever taught us about the dangers of having a poisonous thought life. No one ever explained to us the consequences of looking at life through the filter of a poisoned perception and the deadly impact it could have on our future. No one explained how a poisoned perception could result in broken homes, mediocre marriages, shallow relationships, and ineffective leadership. No one shared how it could result in a life of pain, deep-seated inse-curity, fear and regret, only to get to the end of it all and wonder what life could have been like...

- If we hadn't been so afraid to take some risks and walk by faith.
- If we would have quit making excuses and simply tried.
- If we would have forgiven the people that hurt us.
- If we wouldn't have pushed people away or rejected instruction.
- If we wouldn't have gone through life with such a nega-tive outlook.
- If we would have invested in ourselves, our marriages, and our family more.
- If we would have given ourselves permission to stop trying to impress God and receive His abundant and unearned grace.

A Darkened Lens

In Matthew 6:22-23 (NKJV), Jesus warned of the dangers of a poisoned perception. As I've already pointed out, the enemy knows that he can alter the course of our lives if he can influence the way we see the world around us. Jesus explained it like this:

> "The lamp of the body is the eye. If therefore your eye is good, your whole body will be full of light. But if your eye is bad, your whole body will be full of darkness. If therefore the light that is in you is darkness, how great is that darkness!"

If the lens through which you view the world becomes dark, it will cause everything you look at to seem dark as well. That's why Jesus said, "If therefore the light (or the lens) that is in you is darkness, how great is that darkness." When you have a poi-soned perception, you begin to think that your perspective is the only one that's right, and you can't be told otherwise. You'll become absolutely convinced that you're right and everyone else is wrong, when in reality you've simply begun to view the world through a darkened lens. Again, Satan knows this, and that's why he attempts to introduce all kinds of toxic thoughts into your life. He wants to darken the lens through which you view the world. When he's done that, he's poisoned your perception.

Eight Toxic Traps

While there are a number of things that can alter our view of reality, there are eight primary toxins of which I want to make you aware. Please note: these are *not* the Seven Deadly Thoughts that we will examine in detail in the coming chapters. Nevertheless, they are extremely dangerous and have the ability to poison our perception.

1. **Fear**—When fearful thoughts poison your perception, you'll view change as an enemy to be avoided. Just like the Israelites in the Old Testament, you could waste years going in circles rather than stepping into the will of God for your life.
2. **Fatigue**—Have you ever noticed that when you're tired, your problems look bigger, and you feel smaller? Tired eyes rarely ever see a bright future. This is what fatigue does. It will stop you in your tracks and make molehills look like mountains.
3. **Rejection**—Rejection at any level is painful. If allowed to stick around, the pain from past relationships will poison your perception of yourself and others. It will shake your confidence and cause you to settle for superficial relationships and what feels safe rather than pursue something genuine and wonderful at the risk of being rejected again.
4. **Insecurity**—This is a big one. It's a poison that will cause you to see other people's success as a threat to your own. Insecurity will result in a scarcity mindset deceiving you into believing that there's never enough of anything

to go around. You'll start seeing the world around you through the lens of suspicion and turn everything into an unhealthy competition. The success of others will feel like an attack on your own identity.

5. **Inaccurate Information**–Gossip is one of the deadliest toxins that has ever existed. It takes inaccurate or incomplete information and delivers it to your heart through the poisoned perception of another person. It darkens the lens through which you view other people, places, and things and deals with issues that are often completely out of your control.

6. **Discouragement**–Discouraging voices turn into discouraging thoughts. There's great power in our words, and we don't always realize the impact other people's words have on us. Once discouragement is lodged in our hearts, we tend to build internal walls in our thinking and start to view the world through the lens of "I can't" instead of "I will."

7. **Unforgiveness**–I often say that refusing to forgive someone is like drinking poison and then wishing the person who hurt you would die. When unforgiveness poisons your perception, it will more often than not cause you to see yourself as a permanent victim. You will then spend your life trying to hurt the person that hurt you and taking your pain out on others.

8. **Condemnation** – Believing that God is perpetually angry or disappointed with you will rob you of the peace and joy that Jesus promised. Once you've received the forgiveness of sins through faith in Christ, you're no longer under any form of condemnation – you're now under grace, and you're fully loved and accepted by God. Romans 8:1 says, "There is therefore now no condemnation to those who are in Christ Jesus, who do not walk according to the flesh, but according to the Spirit" (NKJV). All of your sins are forgiven. Though your journey with Jesus has just begun, His love for you is unconditional.

As I said, perception serves as a sort of filter through which you view the world around you. The condition of that filter at the point new information passes through it causes that information to pick up the "flavor" of the filter. If you possess a healthy perception, then everything you see and hear will be processed through a spiritually, intellectually and emotionally healthy filter, enabling you to make the kind of choices that will move you forward, protect your peace and purpose, and lift the limits off your life and leadership. However, if your perception has been poisoned, it will cause you to view everything else around you as poisonous. You'll start to believe that what you perceive is actual reality—even when it's not. Sometimes it's not even in the ball park of truth.

This is why Satan fights so hard for that real estate between your ears. As Jesus pointed out in Matthew 6, a poisoned perception will systematically darken the lens through which you view the world around you. It will cause you to become paranoid and suspicious—oftentimes causing relational paralysis where you can no longer trust anyone. Unconsciously, you will begin to insulate yourself from reality by surrounding yourself only with people who also see the world through an equally "poisoned perception." This deception is so powerful that it can make you "feel" positively right while in reality you are absolutely wrong.

A Poisoned Source

Several years ago I would have bet that most of the world didn't even know that the city of Flint, Michigan, existed. But in 2015 all that changed. Suddenly, the city was thrust into the international spotlight for what became known as the "Flint Water Crisis." Apparently, in an effort to save the city some money, government officials decided to temporarily use the Flint River as the city's new source for drinking water. Unknowingly, they picked the wrong source from which to draw, and it left the residents of Flint drinking from a water source that was poisoned with dangerous levels of lead. Evidently, the lead was picked up from the very pipes through which the water was being delivered. In some cases lead levels in residents' homes tested at seven times higher than the EPA limit.

Every time they turned on their water supply, they were exposed to poison. If they took a shower, they were exposed. If they washed their hands, they were exposed. If they poured water into a mop bucket, they were exposed. Many families in Flint have been forced to drink and/or bathe in bottled water only or advised to use a water filter (though I'm not sure how confident I would personally feel drinking poisoned water through a filter). According to the Mayo Clinic, lead poisoning in children, especially under the age of six, "...can severely affect mental and physical development." It can also cause "... miscarriages in pregnant women, memory loss in adults, and hearing loss in children... Very high lead levels may cause seizures, unconsciousness and possibly death."[9] What's my point?

The effects of having a poisoned perception are much like the effects of drinking from a poisoned water source. We can begin to experience a loss of vision, our future can be miscarried, and our dreams are often put to death. What's even worse, when our perception becomes poisoned, we ourselves often become a tainted source, making those around us sick. Instead of offering others life-giving words, we begin speaking death. Tragically, the uninhibited flow of our toxic words into the hearts and minds of others can become the poison that causes their loss of spiritual vision and hearing, as well as relational miscarriages. Potentially, everyone that draws from us can become a victim of our own poisoned perception.

The healthy people that do manage to stick around someone with a poisoned perception will be forced to put a filter on everything they receive. They simply don't know how much of what is said can actually be trusted because it's all coming from a poisoned source. And just like the tragedy in Flint, which officials are predicting will take years to fix, when a person starts drawing from a poisoned source, it can take a lot of time to repair the resulting damage from a poisoned perception.

The most dangerous aspect of a poisoned perception isn't the way in which you see the world, but the way in which you see yourself. The way you see you is so important that I've devoted an entire chapter to it later on in the book. For now, let's take a look at another dangerous symptom of a poisoned perception.

The Way You *Perceive* Me
Determines the Way You *Receive* Me

In Mark 3, we see Jesus entering a synagogue where He would encounter two very different people who had two very different perceptions of His identity. One was a Pharisee, and the other was a man who needed a miracle. Both of them came to the same church on the same day, but they were each looking for Someone altogether different. One man came looking for a healer, a miracle worker, and a hope dealer. And guess what? He found *exactly* Who he was looking for! The other man came to church looking for a lawbreaker, a sinner, and an instigator. And guess what? He found *exactly* who He was looking for too! Ironically, they both found Who they were looking for in the same Man—Jesus.

How could this be possible? How could they both be looking at the same Jesus and yet see Someone so completely different? Mark 3:2 (NKJV) gives us a clue when the gospel writer reveals *why* the Pharisees were watching Jesus so closely in the first place. He wrote:

> "They watched Him closely...so that they might accuse Him."

It turns out that they were watching Jesus in order to find a reason to *accuse* Him. Why? Because they were looking at life through the lens of a poisoned perception. Think about it for a moment. They watched Jesus—the picture of absolute perfection, the sinless Son of God of Whom the apostle Peter testified had "...COMMITTED NO SIN, NOR WAS ANY DECEIT FOUND IN HIS MOUTH" (1 Peter 2:22 NASB)—yet somehow they managed to find sin in a Man in Whom there was none. They found flaws in Jesus, Who was absolutely perfect, and accused Him—the one and only Man to ever walk the planet Who wasn't accusable.

While many saw Jesus as Savior, all the Pharisees could see was a sinner. Their poisoned perception was so powerful that it caused them to see something that wasn't there. The same holds true for you.

- If you look at your spouse through the lens of *offense*, you'll always find a reason to become offended with them, even when there is none.
- If you view your friends through the lens of *insecurity*, you'll always find a reason to be suspicious of their intentions when there isn't any.
- If you look at others through the lens of *disappointment*, you'll always find another reason to be disappointed.
- If you always look at opportunities through the lens of *fear*, you'll always find a reason to avoid taking any action and instead play it safe.

A darkened lens will cause you to see friends as enemies and enemies as friends. Instead of giving someone the benefit of the doubt, you'll start to doubt the benefit of that relationship. This is why it is so important to pursue and protect a healthy perception. A primary rule of all relationships is:

The way you *perceive* people determines the way you'll *receive* people.

As a matter of fact, we can watch this principle unfold again just three chapters later in Mark 6, when Jesus returned to Nazareth, the town in which He grew up. The Bible says that He was rejected by the people there because they "perceived" Him as being common. They said, "'Is this not the carpenter, the Son of Mary, and brother of James, Joses, Judas, and Simon? And are not His sisters here with us?' So they were *offended* at Him" (v. 3 NKJV).

Please realize there are always consequences of a poisoned perception. The consequences that the people of Nazareth experienced were that Jesus "...could do no mighty work there..." (v.

5). Why? The way the townspeople *perceived* Him was the way they *received* Him. They perceived Jesus as common, ordinary, and nothing special, so that's all they could receive. Their poisoned perception of Jesus prevented them from being able to receive Him as the matchless, miracle-working Son of God. They saw Him as ordinary, so they missed out on the *extraordinary*. They viewed Jesus only in the "natural," so they missed out on the supernatural. Their poisoned perception ruined their visitation with God Himself.

God works "Supernaturally–Naturally," which is just another way of saying that He loves to work through people. This is why Satan tries so hard to poison our perception of the person or relationship through whom God has chosen to deliver on His promises. The enemy knows that the way we perceive one another will determine the way we receive from one another. So he makes it his mission to poison our perception of each other by building walls and creating distance from the very person through whom God is trying to deliver those blessings that we've been waiting for.

- Satan will attempt to drive a wedge between you and your pastor in order to keep you from receiving what God's trying to deliver to you through him.
- He'll attempt to poison your perception of your boss in order to keep you from receiving his leadership training and becoming a better leader yourself.
- He'll attempt to darken the lens through which you see your family in order to rob you of the love and support that you'll need to pursue and fulfill your purpose.
- He'll attempt to poison your perception of your teacher, husband, wife, son, daughter, mother, father, and on and on the list goes.
- He'll try to poison your perception of God so you'll see Him as perpetually angry and indifferent in order to prevent you from trusting Him and walking in His love and purpose for your life.

The bottom line is that the enemy wants to alienate you from the very people that God's trying to bring to you to be a blessing, and he does it by planting deadly thoughts in your mind to poison your perception. If successful, your ability to read people or situations correctly will be repressed. Your ability to process your friends' facial expressions in the middle of an important conversation or interpret the body language of your spouse during an argument will be greatly hindered, transforming an innocent remark into an insult.

So let me ask you: How do you view the world? What is your perception of your relationship with God, your relationship with your boss, and your relationship with your husband or wife? Is it possible that without even knowing it, you are viewing some of the most important relationships or opportunities in your life through a darkened lens? Could it be that you are finding fault in someone where there really is none, or that the fault you see is greatly exaggerated?

The Roar

Under the inspiration of the Holy Spirit, the apostle Peter described one of the tactics that Satan employs in order to poison our perception. He warns us with these words:

> "Stay alert! Watch out for your great enemy, the devil. He prowls around like a roaring lion, looking for someone to devour."

> —1 Peter 5:8 NLT

Please notice that the Bible doesn't say that Satan *is* a roaring lion, but that he prowls around *like* a roaring lion. Why does Satan act like a lion? Because he is the great imitator. He is always creating a counterfeit version of the real thing. In Revelation 5:5, Jesus is called the *Lion* of the tribe of Judah. Consequently, Satan tries to imitate Jesus' authority with his roar. He roars with false authority, attempting to poison the way you see yourself and those around you. He uses this false authority to make something sound true or look true that's not true.

A study was recently conducted where subjects were asked to put on headphones and listen to music. The people controlling the music selections that the subjects were listening to were instructed to play either happy or sad music while those participating simultaneously looked at someone with a neutral facial expression. Participants listening to the music were then asked to describe the mood of the person they were looking at. You can probably predict the results. The subjects who were listening to happy music described the person with the neutral facial expression they were looking at as happy. Conversely, those who were listening to sad music described the person they were looking at as sad. These results reveal an important truth: what we listen to has the power to affect how we see people and the world around us.

This is the strategy of Satan—the false lion, and the timing of his roar is impeccable. You've probably heard the old saying, "When it rains it pours." Sometimes it's really not pouring; it's just sprinkling while the devil is roaring. Listening to his roar can make a sprinkle look like a storm, and he times the sound of his roars like a movie director filming a fight scene. In most fight scenes, there's actually no contact between the people brawling. Although they do swing at each other, they generally come about a foot or two short of actually hitting their opponent. But when the sound editors place the right sound effect in the right place at the right time, what you hear suddenly affects what you see. So, because it sounds like the actors are actually hitting each other, it creates the illusion that they are fighting. That's exactly how the enemy times his roars. For example...

- Have you ever had something go wrong with your kids, and immediately you heard the enemy roar, "You're a terrible parent."
- Have you ever made a mistake at work, and immediately you heard the enemy roar, "You'll never be good enough to get to the next level."

- Maybe you got into an argument with your spouse or a friend, and immediately you heard the enemy roar, "Nothing is ever going to change."

Abraham and Sarah heard the enemy's roar and suffered from a poisoned perception. They no longer believed that God could keep His promises, so they took matters into their own hands. Ten of the twelve spies of Israel heard the roar of the enemy, and their poisoned perception caused them to believe that their enemies were bigger than their God. As a result, they forfeited their opportunity to enter the Promised Land. Likewise, the army of Israel heard the roar of the enemy through the voice of a giant named Goliath. The sound caused all the soldiers to shake in fear and retreat when they heard him speak. The roar of the enemy poisoned the way they perceived themselves, their army, and above all, their God.

In fact, the army of Israel facing Goliath can teach us something about the dangers of entertaining the enemy's roar. Day after day for forty days they listened to the voice of the enemy until the words that he was speaking became the lie that they started believing. In order to defeat the enemy, God had to send someone to fight whose perception hadn't been poisoned. Someone who saw himself as God saw him. Someone who believed that God's promises had the power to defeat the enemy's purpose. So God sent a young shepherd boy named David!

For years, David had filled the silence of those long days tending his earthly father's sheep by singing about his heavenly Father's glory. He meditated on God's promises and recorded them in the Psalms. When David heard the roar of the enemy as spoken through the giant Goliath, those threats couldn't penetrate his pure perception because his heart was so full of faith that there wasn't any room for fear! When David's brothers and King Saul tried to convince him he couldn't win, he responded, "I've been a shepherd, tending sheep for my father. Whenever a lion or bear came and took a lamb from the flock, I'd go after it, knock it down, and rescue the lamb. If it turned on me, I'd grab it by the throat, wring its neck, and kill it. Lion or bear, it made no difference—I killed it. And I'll do the same to this Philistine pig who is taunting the troops of God-Alive. God, who delivered me from the teeth of the lion and the claws of the bear, will deliver me from this Philistine..." (1 Samuel 17:36-37 The MSG).

In essence, David said, "Yeah, I hear the roar of the lion, but I've killed lions like this before." Just as Satan did with David and the army of Israel, he will try very hard to poison your perception through his well-timed, threatening roars. But don't buy in to his lies. Instead, do as David did—cling tightly to the promises of God. His promises have the power to purify your perception.

Purify Your Perception

Just as strongholds have the ability to poison our perception, God's promises have the power to purify it! The Word of God possesses divine *renewing* properties that empower us to live the transformed life the apostle Paul wrote about in Romans 12. God's Word can make our minds brand new all over again. What does the Word do?

- **Ephesians 5:26** (NASB) tells us that we're cleansed "...by the washing of water with the word." So, if we're going to purify our perceptions and start eliminating the enemy's poison, we have to turn our attention to the living Word of God.
- **James 1:21** (AMPC) instructs us to "...receive and welcome the Word which implanted and rooted [in your hearts] contains the power to save your souls." Our soul is our mind, our will, and our emotions. God's Word has the power to literally transform the core of who we are.
- **Hebrews 4:12** (MSG) informs us that "...His powerful Word is sharp as a surgeon's scalpel, cutting through everything, whether doubt or defense, laying us open to listen and obey." When we read and study God's Word, the Word operates on us spiritually, removing that which is diseased and bringing healing we desperately need.

And one of my favorite passages about the Word is found in Psalm 1:2-3 (NASB). In stark contrast to the person who walks in the counsel of the wicked, stands in the path of sinners, and sits in the seat of scoffers, the blessed man's "...delight is in the law of the Lord, and in His law he meditates day and night. He will be like a tree firmly planted by streams of water, which yields its fruit in its season and its leaf does not wither; and in whatever he does, he prospers." According to Psalm 1:2-3, when we begin to meditate, or focus, on God's promises rather than the enemy's poison, the limitations of low thinking no longer have permission to hold us back, and our life and leadership begin to prosper! Where we were once barren and unable to produce, we're suddenly fruitful and growing!

Meditating on God's promises has the power to purify your perception and enable you to:

- See yourself through the eyes of your heavenly Father rather than the poisoned perception of inadequacy, condemnation, or rejection.
- View your marriage and family through the lens of great possibilities and prosperity rather than resentment, regret, and disdain.
- See your future through the lens of divine destiny rather than defeat; have divine purpose rather than meaninglessness; and be an overcomer rather than an underachiever.

The Word of God has the power to purify, heal, restore, and renew. In Psalm 19:7-8 (MSG) the psalmist writes, "The revelation of God is whole and pulls our lives together. The signposts of God are clear and point out the right road. The life-maps of God are right, showing the way to joy. The directions of God are plain and easy on the eyes." Make no mistake. There is nothing in this world that comes close in comparison to the power of God's Word! Psalm 107:20 victoriously declares its healing power. To purify our perception and heal us from the poisonous effects of the enemy's lies, God sends us His Word:

"He sent His word and healed them, and delivered them from their destructions."

—Psalm 107:20 NASB

The poison of the enemy's lies is no match for the power of God's promises! I encourage you to go to the Word daily. Write down the verses that seem to jump off the page, and spend some time meditating on them. God's Word hidden in your heart protects your perception from being poisoned.

Remember that fear, fatigue, rejection, insecurity, incomplete or inaccurate information, discouragement, unforgiveness (pain from past relationships), and condemnation are all potential toxins that can poison your perception. They can contaminate and confuse what's real and what's not, what's true and what's false, and what's right and what's wrong. Once your perception is poisoned, it changes the way you view the world around you, impacting every relationship in your life. It can stifle your career or ministry and disable your marriage and family. A poisoned perception will impede your ability to give and receive love. It will cause you to make emotionally-charged decisions rather than the right decisions; you'll react rather than respond, and it will prevent you from pursuing your purpose and becoming everything God has called and created you to be.

In the next seven chapters, we're going to identify *Seven Deadly Thoughts*—thoughts that if allowed to linger will inevitably result in a poisoned perception. These are the thoughts that the apostle Paul urges us to take "...captive to the obedience of Christ" (2 Corinthians 10:5 NASB). If we don't, they'll not only darken the lens through which we view our relationships and opportunities, but most importantly, they will poison the way we see ourselves.

We're going to slap some of our own bright green "yuck" stickers on the everyday, deadly thoughts that threaten to limit your life and leadership. We're going to identify and, with God's help, tear down some strongholds that threaten to poison your perception of God, yourself, your relationships, and the world around you. I believe that as you open your heart to what God's Spirit is saying, He'll help you to learn to live and lead the abundant life that He's always intended for you.

Chapter 4

"DID GOD REALLY SAY...?"

DEADLY THOUGHT #1: THE STRONGHOLD OF DOUBT

...He who doubts is like a wave of the
sea driven and tossed by the wind.
~James 1:6 (NKJV)

"Our doubts are traitors, and make us lose the
good we oft might win, by fearing to attempt."[10]

~William Shakespeare

The first of the *Seven Deadly Thoughts* can be traced all the way back to the Garden of Eden, and it's just as diabolical today as it was then. This single thought managed to infect the entire human race with the plague of sin—a plague so lethal that it would cause every man and woman ever conceived to crave darkness rather than light, exchange love for lust, and sacrifice their purpose on the altar of momentary pleasure. It would produce a deep-seated doubt within us that God truly loves us and has nothing but good for us.

Peering back into history, we see in Genesis 3 that Satan slithered onto the battlefield of mankind's mind, and using the form of a question, he presented the First Lady of Eden with the atomic bomb of all destructive thoughts:

"...Did God really say..."

—Genesis 3:1 (NIV)

Satan sowed the seed of doubt into Eve's mind. She accepted it, and the rest is history. That was all it took to separate humanity from God—one simple four-word question. When Eve took ownership of that single thought, it immediately "exalted itself against the knowledge of God" (see 2 Corinthians 10:5). She entertained the thought, acted on the thought, and sin entered the human race. Everyone born thereafter would suffer an estranged relationship from their Creator. In that moment, humanity chose mourning rather than joy. We sacrificed beauty to embrace ashes and inherited a legacy of despair rather than the garment of praise.

Eve was so convinced that her actions were right that even after she realized she had sinned, she fed the same deadly thought to her husband, Adam. He believed the lie, too, and took and ate, knowing full well it would do to him what it had done to her. Why would Eve set her husband up for failure? Because sin will open your eyes to a darkness that robs you of the ability to see clearly. A stronghold had been established in Eve's mind—one that convinced her that she knew more and better than God did.

How the Enemy Wields His Weapon

Now, I don't know about you, but this scenario is very sobering to me. It's scary to realize that it's possible to be dead wrong yet be totally convinced that you're absolutely right. Stop and think about how often the enemy utilizes the "Did God really say" question in the vulnerable places of our lives today in order to rob us of the peace and joy that God promises us. Question after question he proposes in our minds, such as:

- *Did God really say that because of Jesus' sacrifice on the cross I'm fully loved and accepted?*

- *Did God really say that ALL of my sins are forgiven — past, present, and future?*
- *Did God really say that He'll never leave me nor forsake me?*
- *Did God really say He's got a plan and purpose for my life?*
- *Did God really say that I need to forgive people that hurt me?*
- *Did God really say we're supposed to pray for those in authority, even if we don't agree with them?*
- *Did God really say there's only one way for man to be saved—through Jesus?*

This list could go on and on, but you get the idea. Satan loves to use the "Did God really say" thought to destroy people's lives. You can be sure that anytime somebody begins to question the authority or authenticity of God's Word with the thought "Did God really say," the enemy is at work waging a war on the battlefield of their mind in order to rob them of the abundant life that Jesus came to give us.

Now, let's bring this destructive thought down to a more personal level. If the enemy wanted to poison your perception of God's purpose for your life, maybe it would sound something like this:

- *Did God really say I should go back to college? After all, I don't even know how I would pay for it.*
- *Did God really say I should stay married? After all, God wants me to be happy, right? And I haven't been happy with him/her for a very long time.*
- *Did God really say I should start a new business or plant a new church? After all, just thinking about it scares me to death, and nobody in my family has ever done anything like that before.*
- *Did God really say I shouldn't marry someone who doesn't love and serve Jesus? After all, maybe God will use me to lead them to Christ after the wedding.*

- *Did God really say that He would never leave me nor forsake me? After all, I've made so many mistakes, how could He possibly still love me?*

All of these are real-life examples of deadly thoughts that the enemy wields against your mind. If not taken captive, they will become a stronghold, preventing you from pursuing your purpose and receiving the abundance of grace that God offers you. Make no mistake about it. This isn't a battle that you or anyone else can avoid. As long as you are alive, you'll face the reality of spiritual combat, and sooner or later you'll have to learn how to cultivate a strategy to take this kind of thought captive and defeat this tactic of the enemy.

When the Going Gets Tough

The temptation to doubt almost always shows up in the face of adversity—when things get really tough in life. The apostle Peter fell prey to the "Did God really say" question in Matthew 14. The Bible says that he and the eleven other disciples were on a boat crossing the Sea of Galilee. They had just watched Jesus take a kid's box lunch consisting of five loaves of bread and two fish and miraculously feed five thousand (not including women and children). This was a miracle moment in the lives of the disciples—a time in which their faith was running high. Typically, this is not when the enemy tries to introduce doubt. He knows that it would be a wasted attack. On the contrary, he almost always launches his assault when we're in the middle of a storm. In times of turmoil and disappointment, we're much more vulnerable to accept the deadly thoughts of doubt and allow them to dominate our thinking. And that's exactly what happened to Peter.

Right after this miraculous meal Jesus had provided, He told His disciples to get into a boat and head to the other side of the lake. At first everything was fine. The water was calm, the stars were shining, and I'm sure the disciples were still slapping high fives, celebrating the amazing things they had just seen Jesus do. What a day! They were on a ministry high, and things couldn't possibly get any better. But a couple of hours into their trip, just as they had started raiding the twelve baskets of leftovers from Jesus' seafood buffet, they heard the sound of rolling thunder in the distance. In that moment, I can imagine Peter looking up from his fish sandwich and asking Thomas, "Hey! What was that?" Seemingly out of nowhere, the Scripture says a storm quickly began to brew, and the disciples were caught in the middle of it.

As the storm raged on for hours, the disciples became exhausted from trying to keep the boat from sinking. The miracle of feeding the five thousand suddenly seemed like a distant memory. Weary from the relentless beating of the wind and the waves, they looked up and saw a fuzzy figure moving toward them on the water. It was Jesus, but they didn't recognize Him at first. They thought He was a ghost and became even more fearful. That's what storms tend to do—they make it hard to recognize the activity of God in and around us.

Knowing they were greatly troubled, Jesus quickly reassured them it was He. "Hey guys, don't sweat it," He said. "It's Me! Don't be afraid." That's when Peter reached out to Jesus in faith.

He said, "Lord, if it is You, command me to come to You on the water" (Matthew 14:28 NKJV). And Jesus said, "Come."

Throwing his legs over the side of the boat, Peter left the other disciples behind and did the impossible—he walked to Jesus *on the water*. But as he made his way to Jesus, something happened. Peter took his eyes off the Lord and began focusing on the storm that was raging. That was the moment he heard the enemy whisper, *"Did Jesus really say, 'Come'?"* As doubt entered Peter his faith started to sink, and so did he. Immediately, the Bible says, Jesus reached out his hand, caught Peter, and said, "O you of little faith, why did you doubt?" (v. 31)

The Dangers of Doubt

A gun has lethal force, but it's not the gun itself that's deadly; it's what comes out of the gun that can kill you. The same is true of our first deadly thought. While the "Did God really say" question is always dangerous when presented by the enemy, it's not

45

the question itself, but rather what is hidden inside of it, that's deadly. The question is just the "Trojan horse," so to speak. It's the vehicle Satan uses to carry the real poison—doubt.

Doubt is the nemesis of faith. It paints an unfinished picture on the canvas of your mind that produces emotional gaps—the kinds of gaps that eventually produce a sense of fear and anxiety in your heart. If doubt is received, like Eve, you'll start to doubt God's will for your life. You'll wonder if He's keeping something good from you or if waiting on the Lord is really the best thing to do. You'll doubt God's love, promises, and commitment to stick with you, even when you fail or make mistakes. You'll also begin questioning your own ability to succeed at fulfilling your purpose. In order to find relief from the sense of uncertainty that doubt always produces, you'll be tempted to fill those gaps quickly by taking matters into your own hands and/or settling for something less than what God created you for. Far too often it's only *after* you've tasted the fruit of doubt that you realize you've been deceived.

As it was for Peter, so it often is for you and me. When we are no longer close to the safety of the shore, when we are too far into something to turn back, that's when the enemy attacks. It's usually in the midst of a storm that doubt knocks on the door of your heart. It comes to convince you that you can't do what God said you can, or that you must have now what God said "not now" to.

Doubt will come knocking on the door of your heart when you're single and tired of watching other people get married. Doubt will start whispering lies when your marriage is under attack and it feels like all you ever do is argue with your spouse. It begins to beat at your mind when money gets tight and you're having a hard time making ends meet, or when your business or ministry isn't growing as fast as you wanted it to. In each of these situations, you'll hear the enemy sigh, *Did God really say..?* It's a thought, or series of thoughts, that comes to offer you the illusion of a shortcut—a way of getting something you want without discomfort, uncertainty, or having to wait on God's timing. See if any of these thoughts sound familiar:

- *Does God really care if I get married to someone that doesn't love Jesus?*
- *Did God really tell me to marry her (or him) in the first place?*
- *Did God really create me with a specific purpose in mind?*
- *Did God really tell me to move to this city and take this job?*
- *Did God really say that you should start this church?*
- *Does God really care how you make money, just as long as you make it?*

James, the half-brother of Jesus, described the dangers of doubt best when he wrote:

> "…He who doubts is like a wave of the sea driven and tossed by the wind. For let not that man suppose that he will receive anything from the Lord; he is a double-minded man, unstable in all his ways."

> ~ James 1:6-8 NKJV

According to this passage, one of the things that makes doubt so dangerous is its ability to divide our mind. Just like a house divided against itself cannot stand (see Mark 3:24-26), so a mind divided against itself *cannot receive anything from the Lord*. It robs us of the peace and joy that Jesus promised and keeps us from hearing God's voice clearly. And when God does speak, we question whether or not it was Him speaking at all because we're listening with a divided mind.

Indecisiveness always reigns in a divided mind. It moves you to make choices based on your circumstances rather than God's promises. When you're faced with having to choose between comfort or your calling, a divided mind will cause you to choose comfort almost every time. Once a stronghold of doubt has been established, all the enemy has to do to get you to change your course or abandon the pursuit of your destiny is stir up one good storm, and you'll start making decisions based upon what feels right rather than what is right.

Doubting God and Yourself

Just like Eve did in the Garden, once a stronghold of doubt is built, you'll start to doubt the very character of God. You'll doubt His ability, His faithfulness, and His love for you. You'll begin questioning His plan for your life and His ability to see you through your dark season and deliver on His promises. Satan will use a storm of grief to get you to question whether or not God is truly good. He'll use your apparent lack of provision to get you to doubt God's faithfulness as your Provider. He'll use your past to poison your perception of God's ability to protect your future. He'll use your brokenness to get you to doubt God's love and His desire to bless you. He'll exploit your weaknesses to get you to doubt God's strength.

If you don't take the enemy's thoughts of doubt captive, the stronghold in your mind will intensify, causing you to begin taking matters into your own hands. Rather than trusting God for the pace of His plan to unfold, you'll try to make things happen yourself. Abraham and Sarah give us a perfect example of what happens when we employ the *do it yourself* (DIY) mentality. It's messy, it delays God's plan, and it often creates unwanted consequences for years to come (see Genesis 16:1-16; 21:8-21).

As the *"Did God really say"* question expands its grip, you move from doubting God to also doubting yourself. You start thinking and saying things like, "This is just too hard;" "I can't do this anymore;" or "What in the world was I thinking!? This dream is way too big for me."

In Chapter 2, we learned that the way we *think* and the way we *act* are inseparably connected to one another. Through the apostle James, God not only confirms this truth, but also adds an entirely new aspect to it. He says that the man who doubts is "...a double-minded man, unstable in *all* his ways" (James 1:8 NKJV). Therefore, if our minds are filled with doubts about God and ourselves, we are going to become mentally and emotionally unstable, doubting things in every area of our lives. So, is there a way out of this downward spiral? The answer is, yes!

God's Proven Plan of Attack to Defeat Doubt

Without question, Satan has been highly successful for thousands of years using his *"Did God really say?"* line of thinking. However, it is not foolproof. In fact, there was One Person he attempted to use this attack on Who stood through the test and showed us the winning strategy to defeat the devil – Jesus! His encounter with Satan is documented in detail in two of the gospels. Recalling the tempter's second wave of attack against the Lord, Matthew wrote:

> "Next the devil took him to the peak of a very high mountain and showed him all the kingdoms of the world and their glory. 'I will give it all to you,' he said, 'if you will kneel down and worship me.'"

> —Matthew 4:8-9 NLT

Can you hear it? It's subtle, but it's there. Although Satan didn't come right out and use the exact *"Did God really say"* verbiage, you can still hear it implied in his proposition to Jesus. He implied in the form of a shortcut:

> "Did God really say You'd have to suffer and die to be King of Kings and Lord of Lords? Did God really say that the cross was needed in order for You to inherit the earth? I can give it all to You right now, and You won't have to wait. All You need to do is bow down and worship me..."

Satan offered Jesus a shortcut that bypassed the cross. But there was a price—bowing down and worshiping him. The enemy's requirements have not changed. Any time he offers us a shortcut and we take it, you'd better believe it's going to cost us something. In some way, shape, or form, we will be obligated to bow down to his plan and abandon God's will for our lives.

The moment Jesus was tempted, He felt the same tug of sin on His heart that we do. The deadly arrows of doubt were being fired against His mind. The crucifixion that awaited didn't excite Jesus at all. According to Scripture, He would have preferred to save mankind another way if it were available—a way that didn't involve His death on a cross (Matthew 26:39).

How did Jesus respond when He heard the enemy's doubts and felt the pull of his enticing shortcut? He made a decision: He chose to believe His heavenly Father in spite of how He felt and what was going on around Him! And through Jesus' actions we can learn how to pull down the stronghold of doubt in our own lives. The Bible reveals that every time the enemy came against Jesus, He turned to the Word of God and declared:

> "Get out of here, Satan,... For the Scriptures say, 'You must worship the Lord your God and serve only him.' Then the devil went away, and angels came and took care of Jesus."

> —Matthew 4:10-11 NLT

Using the scripture, Jesus took the deadly thoughts of doubt captive! And when Jesus focused on the Word of God rather than the lies of the enemy, the devil "went away"! Do you want to take the deadly thought of doubt captive to the obedience of Christ? Then do what Jesus did—turn to the Word of God. *Know* the Word, and *declare* the Word!

Second Corinthians 1:20 (NIV) tells us that "...no matter how many promises God has made, they are 'Yes' in Christ..." So the next time the enemy attempts to inject his doubts and establish a stronghold in your mind by asking you the *"Did God really say"* question, take his thoughts captive with that truth!

If the enemy whispers:

- *Did God really say you can be healed?* You answer, "Absolutely! The promises of God are all yes in Christ!"
- *Did God really say your marriage can be made whole?* You answer, "Yes! 'God is not a man, so he does not lie. He is not human, so he does not change his mind...'" (Numbers 23:19 NLT).
- *Did God really say He'd come through for you?* You answer, "Yes, He will come through! '...The LORD...God is God; he is the faithful God, keeping his covenant of love to a thousand generations of those who love him...'" (Deuteronomy 7:9 NIV).

Oh, there is one more thing I want to mention to help you defeat doubt: build godly relationships with others who have received the Gospel. There's dynamic power when two or more come together and agree in prayer, and the encouragement of a brother or sister in Christ is priceless! Ecclesiastes 4:12 (NLT) tells us:

> "A person standing alone can be attacked and defeated, but two can stand back-to-back and conquer. Three are even better, for a triple-braided cord is not easily broken."

If you're going to take every thought captive and destroy the stronghold of doubt, you're going to need life-giving Christ-centered relationships; one or two people who will be there for you when you're fighting this attack can make all the difference in the world. These are people who believe in the power of God's Word to destroy the lies of the enemy—godly friends you can trust who will stand back-to-back with you to fight the devil with prayer and the Word.

If you're married, one of these people can be your spouse. Whoever you choose, it should be someone you can be honest and open with about your battles—someone who won't judge you because you're being tempted but will instead believe the best in you. I've discovered that this type of accountability is a gift, especially when we're going through a tough time.

So when the enemy comes against you with his *"Did God really say"* doubts, stand against him and say, "Get out of here, Satan! This storm will not dictate my destiny. My mind is made up. I trust in the Lord, and I will put my faith in His Word. Just like Jesus, I'm going to focus on the joy set before me. Greater things are coming, in Jesus' name!"

TAKING IT CAPTIVE:

1 – The enemy is skilled at bringing doubt against you. Therefore, you must learn to be skilled to stand against him with truth. Below are three main areas in which the enemy tries to get you to doubt, along with a few scriptures refuting his lies. Look up each verse. Jot down what God is showing you, and write out at least two of the verses that you find most encouraging.

Did God really say the Bible is His Word? Can It really be trusted?
2 Timothy 3:16-17 • 2 Peter 1:20-21• Psalm 119:89 • Isaiah 40:8 • Hebrews 4:12

I believe God is showing me through these passages...

_____

_____

_____

_____

_____

The verses that encourage me most are...

_____

_____

_____

_____

_____

Did God really say that He loves you? Will He always love you? What about when you mess up?
Romans 5:8; 8:31-39 • 1 John 3:19-22 • John 3:16-20 • 1 John 1:9 • Psalm 103:12

I believe God is showing me through these passages...

_____

_____

_____

_____

_____

The verses that encourage me most are...

_____

_____

_____

_____

_____

2 – Godly friends are priceless! They don't condemn us if we fail, but they also don't condone our wrong behavior. Name one or two people you are doing life with right now who are a *strength* and an *encouragement* to you in your walk with God. Briefly describe your relationship with them, and tell what you appreciate most about them.

_____

_____

_____

_____

_____

KEY SCRIPTURES ON THE VALUE OF FRIENDSHIPS: Proverbs 17:17; 27:10,17; Ecclesiastes 4:9-10.

Chapter 5

"I DON'T HAVE WHAT IT TAKES"

DEADLY THOUGHT #2: THE STRONGHOLD OF INSECURITY

Although you may think little of yourself,
are you not the leader...
~1 Samuel 15:17 NLT

"...I often notice a striking similarity [among leaders]: many of them live with a significant measure of insecurity. It shows up in comparison, competition, and flashes of self-doubt. I've learned to recognize this often-buried but common trait in leaders because I've struggled with it myself."[11]

~ Dr. Sam Chand

"I Don't Have What It Takes." This lie is fueled by fear and rooted in the stronghold of insecurity. *Insecurity* is defined by Merriam Webster's Dictionary as "a lack of confidence or assurance; a state of instability." The truth is we all deal with insecurity in one form or another. We make mistakes, people hurt us – life happens.

When we don't process our painful feelings in a manner that's healthy, our perception of ourselves becomes poisoned. As a result, insecurity takes root, and we begin to accumulate all kinds of baggage in our lives. Ironically, it's usually not insecurity itself that creates the baggage. It's all of the unhealthy ways we attempt to cope with insecurity that produces baggage and causes it to multiply.

Check out this list of symptoms or "baggage" that is created from not confronting our insecurity. You'll notice that insecurity often manifests in opposite extremes:

- Insecurity can cause someone to stay single for the rest of their lives, or it can motivate them to pursue multiple affairs after they're married.
- Insecurity can cause a person to constantly brag about themselves, or it can make them never talk about themselves at all (aka false humility).
- In the face of competition, the presence of insecurity will often move a person to *isolate* (quit) or *dominate* (try to make other people quit).
- Insecurity can cause someone to either hate being in front of a camera or become a camera hog (and will even get angry if they aren't included in a picture). Can you say "selfie"?
- Insecurity creates a lack of identity which causes people to frequently attempt to *imitate* others or try to *intimidate* others.
- Insecure people will often either beg for attention or resent it.
- Insecurity will prevent a person from admitting when they're wrong (for fear of being seen as weak), or it will persuade them to always take the blame, even when it's not their fault (because they want to be liked and accepted).

Moreover, insecurity is the mother of two not-so-wonderful wonder twins: *pride* and *fear*. Wherever insecurity exists, pride and fear will always be close by, attempting to keep watch over the wounded areas of our lives. Their goal is to keep us from being wounded again, but what they actually end up doing is preventing our healing. Insecurity is the oxygen that pride and fear need to survive in our lives. When insecurity is confronted, pride and fear feel threatened and will fight to stay in control.

Keep in mind it's not the baggage that will determine our outcome in life or in our leadership, for that matter. It's what we choose to do with the baggage that determines our ability to fulfill our God-ordained destiny.

If you refuse to deal with it head-on, then whenever a God-ordained opportunity comes your way, the presence of unchecked insecurity in your life will cause you to hide among your own baggage, which is exactly what we see happening in the life of a man named Saul.

King Saul: An Image of Insecurity

Probably no person in the Bible so clearly personifies insecurity like King Saul. His life demonstrates the dangers of *low thinking.* He was handpicked by God to become the first king of Israel. Standing head and shoulders above the rest, Saul was the son of his very wealthy and affluent father Kish. No doubt this resulted in privileged access to the kind of high-quality people, places, and things that were normally afforded to a man of substance. Indeed, he had the finest education, clothes and houses that money could buy.

The Bible says that Saul became one of the most skilled military leaders in the entire Israelite army, which brought its own kind of fame. His amazing victories on the battlefield catapulted Saul to rockstar status, moving the people to write and sing songs about him with choruses like, "Saul has killed his thousands!" Apparently, when a sword was placed in Saul's hand, he turned into the Gladiator/James Bond/Terminator of combat. In short, Saul was the man!

On top of all this, Saul was most likely pretty popular with the ladies. The Scripture records "...Saul was the most handsome man in Israel—head and shoulders taller than anyone else in the land" (1 Samuel 9:2 NLT). Basically, Saul's Linked-In Bio might have read:

> Son of a wealthy CEO. Set to inherit father's fortune. Military combat expert. Medal of Honor recipient. Multiple Mr. Universe titles. Voted Most Likely to Succeed. Selected as Most Eligible Bachelor in the Country. Ivy League graduate with the most prestigious job in the world on deck—First King of Israel. YOLO!

Saul appeared to have everything a person would need in order to become a legendary, high-level leader: money, power, charisma, fame, and above all else, he was chosen by God to hold the highest rank of leadership in the entire nation. Yet when it came time for Saul to officially step into his destiny and be crowned king, the Bible says that he actually went MIA. Specifically it says, "...when they looked for him, he had disappeared" (1 Samuel 10:21 NLT).

After the people had searched everywhere they knew to look, they prayed and asked God to show them where Saul was. And guess what? That's just what God did (talk about enabling your location services!). God's revelation of Saul's whereabouts is when things start to get a little confusing. For when they asked God for the location of this amazingly gifted, talented, and attractive leader, the Lord said:

> "...He is hiding among the baggage."

> **—1 Samuel 10:22 (NLT)**

I can just imagine what the people were thinking. *The baggage, God? Did You just say Saul, "The Man," is hiding among the baggage? How can this be possible?* It certainly was puzzling. How could a man who was so gifted and chosen—a man with so much power and fame and so highly thought of by both God and man—be found hiding from his own purpose among the baggage? I believe the answer to this question can be found five chapters later in 1 Samuel 15:17 (NLT) where the prophet Samuel confronted Saul about not fully obeying God's instructions. He said:

> "Although *you may think little of yourself*, are you not the leader of the tribes of Israel? The Lord has anointed you king of Israel."

Saul's perception of himself had been poisoned. The problem wasn't with how God or the people thought of Saul. The issue was with how *Saul* thought about Saul. As it turns out, the entire time he was swinging his sword and building his leadership resume, he also was fighting a battle within that no one else could see—a battle against an enemy called insecurity.

And Saul was losing.

Frozen in Fear

Coronation day may have been the first time Saul hid among his baggage, but it wasn't the only time. The more he allowed time to pass without confronting his insecurities, the less he thought of himself, and the more insecurity had control over his life. Eventually, Saul became merely a shadow of the man he once was and barely a glimpse of the man that he could have become.

Like any person who fails to confront his insecurity, Saul often became frozen in the face of conflict or adversity. Rather than risk making the wrong decision, he wouldn't make any decision at all. His insecurity manifested in indecisiveness as it often does. First Samuel 17 records the popular account of the time King Saul led his entire army out to fight against the Philistines and encountered the mighty giant from Gath. Once he set up camp, Scripture says,

> "Saul countered by gathering his Israelite troops near the valley of Elah. So the Philistines and Israelites faced each other on opposite hills, with the valley between them. Then Goliath, a Philistine champion from Gath, came out of the Philistine ranks to face the forces of Israel. He was over nine feet tall!"

> **—1 Samuel 17:2-4 (NLT)**

When you continue reading the rest of the story, you'll discover that Saul led his army *to* the battle, but not *into* the battle. His insecurity led to indecisiveness. The presence of insecurity will cause even the best of us to leave the most important things in life unfinished. We'll know what needs to be done but struggle to find the courage to do it for fear of failure. Insecurity poisons our perception so much that *looking good* becomes more appealing than doing good. Think about that for a moment; Saul went from being a mighty soldier and leader on the battlefield who was "killing his thousands" to one avoiding conflict at all costs.

For Saul, everything seemed fine until the giant named Goliath changed the rules of the game. Instead of the customary army against army combat, Goliath challenged Saul to send over his best soldier for a duel, and whoever won the duel, won the war. The fact that Saul, the king who had been handpicked by God, allowed the enemy to change the rules in the first place proves that he had forgotten *who* he was and *Whose* he was. In reality, the most dangerous giant in Saul's life wasn't the one standing in front of him — it was the one living inside of him. It was the giant of insecurity that kept telling him, *You don't have what it takes.*

For forty days and forty nights, Goliath's taunting continued. Every morning and evening he would come out from among his ranks and shout insults across the valley at the Israelite army. The entire time we don't hear so much as a peep from Saul. The irony is that while Saul refused to make a move for fear that he'd lose the battle and be taken captive by the enemy, he had already been taken captive by a poisoned perception.

This same principle holds true for you and me. No matter how gifted, talented, or well-liked we are, the presence of insecurity has the power to sabotage our lives if we don't stand against it. It doesn't matter if we go back to school and acquire a second master's degree or if we change churches, jobs, cities, or even spouses. Until you and I confront our insecurities, we'll always find ourselves hiding among our baggage, thinking, *I don't have what it takes,* and we'll spend our lives trying to prove to everyone that we do.

Make no mistake. Insecurity is like an obnoxious, uninvited house guest that won't leave on its own. The only way to get it out of your life is to confront it head-on. This, however, is where things can get kind of tricky, because insecurity, by its very nature, *does not* want to be confronted and will avoid confrontation at all costs. It will do whatever it takes to remain in the dark corners of your life and avoid any unpleasant encounter that may shed light on its presence.

In his book *The Emotionally Healthy Leader*, author Peter Scazzero refers to this need to confront our insecurities as "Facing Your Shadow." He writes:

> "Your shadow is the accumulation of untamed emotions, less-than-pure motives and thoughts that, while largely unconscious, strongly influence and shape your behaviors. It is the damaged but mostly hidden version of who you are. The shadow may erupt in various forms. Sometimes it reveals itself in sinful behaviors, such as judgmental perfectionism, outbursts of anger, jealousy, resentment, lust, greed, or bitterness. Or it may reveal itself more subtly through a need to rescue others and be liked by people, a need to be noticed, an inability to stop working, a tendency toward isolation, or rigidity. Aspects of the shadow may be sinful, but they may also simply be weaknesses or wounds. They tend to appear in the ways we try to protect ourselves from feeling vulnerable or exposed."[12]

The presence of insecurity will often cause you to look for fulfillment in the next award, achievement, or accomplishment in order to block out or erase the overwhelming feeling of uncertainty that keeps gnawing away at your mind. The truth is, however, titles, promotions, or extra attention won't get insecurity out of the driver's seat of your life. In fact, most of the time those things only serve to feed your insecurities and magnify the problem.

By the way, running from your insecurities is not an option either. Yes, you can move to another city, but the problem remains because you take *you* with you wherever you go. If you want to conquer the shadows of low thinking, then you've got to give God permission to confront them, and then surrender to His healing process.

Confronting Your Enemy

After Saul had spent forty days and nights hiding among the baggage, the Lord sent a young, short, and inexperienced shepherd boy named David to the battle line. Initially, David didn't know he was going there to fight, but the moment he heard Goliath shouting insults across the valley, he was moved to action. That's what happens when we really know how much God loves us and is for us. We don't waver or wait around. We take action, knowing God, our Rock, is with us, and we will not be moved (see Psalm 62:2, 6).

Unlike King Saul, David took the field of battle on the same day he heard Goliath's threats. Ironically, he wasn't armed with a sword or shield. All he had in his hands to fight Goliath was a sling and a stone. Even when the nine foot tall giant cursed David and shouted insults directly at him, David refused to be intimidated. Take a look at how the scene unfolded:

> "Goliath walked out toward David with his shield bearer ahead of him, sneering in contempt at this ruddy-faced boy. 'Am I a dog,' he roared at David, 'that you come at me with a stick?' And he cursed David by the names of his gods. 'Come over here, and I'll give your flesh to the birds and wild animals!' Goliath yelled.

> "David replied to the Philistine, 'You come to me with sword, spear, and javelin, but I come to you

in the name of the Lord of Heaven's Armies—the God of the armies of Israel, whom you have defied. Today the Lord will conquer you, and I will kill you and cut off your head. And then I will give the dead bodies of your men to the birds and wild animals, and the whole world will know that there is a God in Israel! And everyone assembled here will know that the Lord rescues his people, but not with sword and spear. This is the Lord's battle, and he will give you to us!'"

—1 Samuel 17:41-47 (NLT)

David didn't play it safe. Despite the fact that King Saul, Goliath, and even his brothers, offered a ton of trash talk in order to convince him that he couldn't defeat his enemy, David refused to let any of them talk him out of his purpose. Though smaller, less equipped, and less experienced, he managed to kill the giant in one shot. That's the power of thinking higher thoughts! David thought highly of his God, and by default he thought more highly of himself. He knew who his God was, and, therefore, he knew who he was. This is evident throughout many of the Psalms he wrote, including the first three verses in Psalm 27 (NASB):

> "The Lord is my light and my salvation; whom shall I fear? The Lord is the defense of my life; whom shall I dread? When evildoers came upon me to devour my flesh, my adversaries and my enemies, they stumbled and fell. Though a host encamp against me, my heart will not fear..."

David—the short, ruddy, and unassuming shepherd boy who found his identity and security in the Lord—managed to do in one day what Saul hadn't been able to do in forty. With faith in God he declared, "In your strength I can crush an army; with my God I can scale any wall" (2 Samuel 22:30 NLT). That's the power of thinking higher thoughts!

Yet despite his amazing victory over Goliath, don't think for a moment that David didn't struggle with baggage of his own. The Bible reveals that David wasn't just the runt of the litter of eight, but he was also often misunderstood and antagonized by his brothers. What's worse, his own father didn't believe in or affirm him. Nevertheless, David did not let their treatment keep him from fulfilling his calling.

Interestingly, just before young David took the field of battle against Goliath, he did something that I believe changed the game and gave him the upper hand. Scripture says:

> "Then David left his baggage in the care of the baggage keeper, and ran to the battle line..."

> **—1 Samuel 17:22 (NASB)**

David *left his baggage with the baggage keeper.* Please don't read past that verse too quickly. Although the verse applies to the physical baggage he was carrying, there is spiritual significance in this statement. David couldn't go into battle carrying the extra weight of bitterness, offense, fear and insecurity, so he made the choice to let it all go. By doing so, he purified his perception and positioned himself to walk in victory.

God Cures the Insecure

Without question, God wants to heal and set free every person held prisoner by insecurity. Interestingly, He has a track record of simultaneously calling people to pursue their purpose and healing them as they walk it out. This means that you don't have to wait until you're perfectly whole to step into your destiny and begin accomplishing amazing things for the glory of God. He can do great things in and through you right here, right now!

There are countless men and women in Scripture who were no strangers to insecurity and its baggage. Yet each and every time they surrendered themselves to God and His process of healing their insecurity, they left their baggage with the Baggage

Keeper and achieved victories in their lives that at one time seemed impossible. Can you relate to any of these people?

God Chose Moses

God chose Moses to lead His people out of captivity after 400 years of backbreaking bondage. While at first glance you may think he had it all together, he did not. Like others, Moses had a poisoned perception of who he was. He saw himself as a poor leader and a less than capable public speaker. In fact, his low thinking was so deeply rooted that he actually argued with God about His calling:

> "But Moses said to God, 'Who am I, that I should go to Pharaoh...'"

> **—Exodus 3:11 (NASB)**

> "Then Moses said, 'What if they will not believe me or listen to what I say? For they may say, "The Lord has not appeared to you."'"

> **—Exodus 4:1 (NASB)**

> "Then Moses said to the Lord, 'Please, Lord, I have never been eloquent, neither recently nor in time past, nor since You have spoken to Your servant; for I am slow of speech and slow of tongue.'"

> **—Exodus 4:10 (NASB)**

Again and again, Moses' words revealed his struggle with insecurity. Yet God did not wait until Moses was soaring with confidence to work through his life and release him to walk in his own God-given purpose. On the contrary, God took him right then and there and began to work in Moses and through Moses. It is in our weaknesses that God is visibly the strongest (see 2 Corinthians 12:9).

Like Moses, insecurity will try to get you to believe that God either picked the wrong person for the job or picked the wrong job for the person. However, what God has called you to do reveals what He put inside of you. As you read through the Scriptures, you'll see Moses eventually came to the point where he left his baggage with the Baggage Keeper. He confronted Pharaoh, who was perhaps the most powerful leader in the world at that time, and led 1.5 million people out of Egyptian captivity. That's the power of leaving your baggage with the Baggage Keeper!

God Chose Peter

What comes to mind when you think of Peter? Sure, he was bold, rugged, and straightforward in his communication. However, he too dealt with insecurity. He had a tendency to open his mouth when he should have kept quiet and remain quiet when he should have opened his mouth. When the pressure was on, he was so insecure about his identity that he denied even knowing Jesus three separate times in order to fit in with the crowd.

By the time Jesus was resurrected and met Peter on the beach, Peter was so overloaded with baggage that he could hardly bear it. He had turned his back on Jesus and retreated to his old way of life—fishing. How did Jesus respond? Did He verbally tear Peter down? Did He give him the silent treatment and only talk with the other disciples? No. Jesus met Peter right where he was in his condition of brokenness. He took Peter's baggage and restored him to his rightful place in ministry.

Peter would subsequently become the spokesman for the Church. His first Spirit-filled sermon was preached to literally thousands of people, and 3,000 of them were so cut to the heart that they put their faith in Jesus as a result. What had changed? What happened? How could a guy be so insecure that he denied Christ in front of a few casual acquaintances one day and suddenly preached Christ in front of thousands of strangers on another day? The answer: Peter left his baggage with the Baggage Keeper.

God Chose Mary

Then there was Mary—a poor girl from a poor town who was visited by the archangel Gabriel. Upon appearing, the angel said, "'...Greetings favored woman! The Lord is with you!' Confused and disturbed, Mary tried to think what the angel could mean" (Luke 1:28-29 NLT). She was young and clearly insecure in her own identity. After hearing the angel's greeting, she was greatly disturbed and thought, *Perhaps he is talking to the wrong Mary*.

In the very next sentence, God used Gabriel to speak directly to her insecurity saying, "...Do not be afraid, Mary; for you have found favor with God. And behold, you will conceive in your womb and bear a son, and you shall name Him Jesus" (Luke 1:30-31 NASB). With her assignment now revealed, insecurity again tried to cloud her thoughts in the form of doubt.

"'But how can this happen? I am a virgin" (Luke 1:34 NLT). Shaken to the core by his words, Mary begins to unknowingly question her own purpose. Let me offer my interpretation of what was likely going through Mary's mind: *How can this happen? I don't have what it takes. I don't even have a husband. I've never done this before. Are you sure you picked the right person?*

But in verse 38, Mary decided to leave her baggage with the Baggage Keeper and declared, "'I am the Lord's servant. May everything you have said about me come true.'" In other words, "I'm a little freaked out, and I have no idea how this is going to work. But I'm going to step into it anyway and trust God with the outcome."

Essentially, Mary chose to see herself the way God saw her. She gives us a picture of what it means to genuinely trust God when what we see and understand about life makes no sense.

There's Hope for You!

How about you? What giants are in your life that you need to defeat? What would your life be like if you traded a poisoned perception for a pure one? How would your marriage, your relationships with your children, your career, or your ministry look if you made up your mind that your past is no longer going to keep you from your future? What would your life be like if you got rid of all your baggage and gave yourself permission to believe that God loves you, accepts you, and favors you right now?

There is hope for you! Jesus is willing to be your Baggage Keeper. He is no respecter of persons. What He did for David and countless others, He'll also do for you. In Matthew 11:28 (NLT) Jesus said,

> "'Come to me, all of you who are weary and carry
> heavy burdens, and I will give you rest.'"

It doesn't matter what kind of baggage you've been carrying, the amount of messes that you've made, or the number of insecurities you've spent years trying to keep hidden. In spite of it all, Jesus is still calling you to fulfill your purpose. He is waiting for you to hand over the pain and the heavy burdens that have collected in your life as a direct result of the stronghold of insecurity. Reject the enemy's lie of *I don't have what it takes*. Let Jesus purify your perception of how you see yourself and Him. Your insecurities don't have to hold you back another day. Today you can begin accomplishing your purpose and choose to surrender to God's healing process in your life.

You Have What It Takes!

I can't close out this chapter without telling you what you've been waiting to hear: **You have what it takes** to be who God created you to be and do what God created you to do. But don't just take my word for it. Look at what your Creator has to say about you:

"I knew you before I formed you in your mother's womb. Before you were born I set you apart..."

—Jeremiah 1:5 (NLT)

You've been set apart for a special purpose. Under the inspiration of the Holy Spirit, the apostle Paul confirmed this reality when he wrote in Ephesians 2:10 (NLT):

"For we are God's masterpiece. He has created us anew in Christ Jesus, so *we can do* the good things he planned for us long ago."

You were created on purpose, with purpose. When you surrendered your life to God and He birthed you into His family, He provided everything you need to fulfill your destiny. Through Peter, He declares:

"*Everything* that goes into a life of pleasing God has been miraculously given to us by getting to know, personally and intimately, the One who invited us to God. The best invitation we ever received!"

—2 Peter 1:3 MSG

You do have what it takes to do what God has called you to do because His Spirit is living in you. The treasure of who you are may currently be hidden from your sight, but it's not hidden from God's sight. Rest assured that He is more than able to unearth what's inside of you. Whatever appears to be missing, God will provide at the right time. God has nothing but good for you, and He sees nothing but the best in you. Your value in God's eyes will never change or diminish. You are accepted by God the Father, and He promises to never leave you or withdraw His love from you. You can do all things through Christ Who gives you strength!

Taking it Captive:

1 – Take a few minutes to read back over the list of symptoms/baggage that results from not confronting insecurity. Which one(s) do you identify with most? Why do you think this is the case?

_____

_____

_____

_____

_____

2 – We all have baggage, and the enemy tries to provide us with more every day. There is only one thing to do with our baggage, and these verses reveal it. Take a few moments and meditate on these instructions from God. What new, God-blessed response can you develop from these scriptures?

1 Peter 5:7 • Philippians 4:6-8 • Matthew 11:28-30 • Psalm 37:5 • Proverbs 16:3
My NEW RESPONSE to thoughts and feelings of insecurity is...

_____

_____

_____

_____

_____

3 – Saul's insecurity manifested in *indecisiveness*. Rather than make a wrong decision, he made no decision at all. Has indecisiveness been an issue for you? If so, in what areas? What is the Lord showing you about that tendency through this chapter?

_____

_____

_____

_____

_____

4 – *Self-confidence* is really overrated. The real winners in this life and the one to come are those who place their *confidence in God*. Take time to look up these promises from God's Word. What is He showing you in these verses—about trusting in *yourself* and *others* versus trusting in Him?

Psalm 118:5-9; 146:3-6 • Proverbs 3:5-8, 25-26; 28:26; 29:25 • Jeremiah 17:5-8 • Isaiah 2:22; 26:3
I believe God is showing me through these passages...

_____

_____

_____

_____

_____

5 – How do you see yourself? God wants you to see yourself as HE sees you—*in Christ*. Check out these key verses revealing your new identity *in Christ*. Write out the one that energizes you most, and commit it to memory.

2 Corinthians 5:21 • Ephesians 1:3-13 • Romans 8:1-2

_____

_____

_____

_____

_____

For a deeper study, search the phrase "in Christ" in a Bible search engine to get an even greater understanding of your identity in Him!

Chapter 6

"I HAVE ARRIVED"

DEADLY THOUGHT #3: THE STRONGHOLD OF PRIDE

The pride of your heart has deceived you...
~Obadiah 1:3 (NIV)

"...If we are motivated by pride, we will resent any implication that we are weak or any revelation that shows our failings."[13]

~ Gary Thomas

The third deadly thought we need to be aware of is directly linked with the stronghold of pride. If Satan can't pull you down, he'll try to puff you up. Perhaps the only thought more dangerous than the thought *I can never be good enough* is the thought *I have arrived!* Now let me be clear here, I'm not talking about your standing with God. The moment you put your faith in Jesus, you are in good standing with the Lord. In fact, the Bible says, "Because of our faith, Christ has brought us into this place of undeserved privilege where we now stand, and we confidently and joyfully look forward to sharing God's glory" (Romans 5:2 NLT). Because of what Jesus accomplished on the cross, God's not asking you to impress Him, He's simply asking you to trust Him—to trust that Jesus finished the work on the cross so that all you have to do is place your faith in Him, and you will be saved and accepted. The stronghold that I'm talking about is the kind that will convince you that you have nothing left to learn. It often renders people unteachable, arrogant, and difficult to know.

Regardless of your position in life—single or married, pastor, parent, or CEO—pride is to your soul and spirit what cancer is to your body. It's deadly. The longer it lingers, the more it grows, and like cancer, the longer pride goes undetected, the harder it is to remove without causing serious damage.

Pride is a disease that initiates its attacks on your eyes and ears—it removes your ability to see when it's present and causes you to refuse to hear the warnings of others that it is operating in your life. I've heard it said that pride is the only disease known to man where everyone is aware of its presence except for the one who has it. It can turn your thoughts against you, convincing you that you're right, and everyone else is wrong.

The prophet Obadiah said, "The pride of your heart has deceived you..." (Obadiah 1:3 NIV). Pride wants you to believe the thought, *I have arrived. I know it all.* However, the truth is, learning is a lifelong pursuit. In the words of legendary UCLA basketball coach John Wooden, "When you're through learning, you're through." I always tell young college graduates, "Your degree is something to celebrate. But remember, the only thing that degree proves is what you've learned so far. It's not a license to stop learning."

As you begin this chapter, make the choice to be open to what the Holy Spirit wants to show you. His wisdom and insights are life-giving when you receive and act on them.

Pride Is Intoxicating

The effect of pride on a person's life is powerful. It will cause you to become drunk on your own opinion of yourself, inhibiting your ability to discern fantasy from reality regarding your own abilities. In the natural, drunkenness can cause you to make poor choices. It will make you believe that you can do something you can't (or shouldn't). One of the reasons drinking and driving is so dangerous is that it impairs your vision. It inhibits your ability to see what's around you or even what's right in front of you. As a result, you not only risk hurting yourself, but also those around you. The same holds true for pride. Marriages, ministries and companies have fallen apart because people allowed themselves to become drunk with pride.

A prideful heart will only allow relationships with those that feed it praise, telling it what it wants to hear and that it's always right. The prouder you become, the more you'll speak about yourself rather than God—you'll make a bigger deal about your own presence than God's presence. In fact, pride eventually repels and replaces God's presence with self-worship.

In the context of leadership, being intoxicated with pride will almost always cause you to think you're ready to do something before you really are. Describing one of the most well-known leaders in the Old Testament, author and pastor Phil Pringle points us to Moses as he addresses the need to eliminate pride in our lives. He wrote:

> "When Moses thought he was ready, he wasn't. When he thought he wasn't, he was. The heart ambitious to lead is a poor foundation for great leadership. No leader should be too hungry for the job. We lead because we are called to lead."[14]

Walking in pride is perhaps the quickest way to ensure that you find a place on God's shelf, waiting and wanting to be used to the fullest measure of your potential. While in your heart you know that you were created for something more, you're unable to experience it because pride has become the lid that has capped the potential in your life. Recognizing the dangers of pride, Paul wrote to the church in Rome, and to us, and said:

> "For I say, through the grace given to me, to everyone who is among you, not to think of himself more highly than he ought to think, but to think soberly..."

—Romans 12:3 (NKJV)

Are you thinking *soberly* about yourself, or has the intoxication of pride poisoned your perception? This is a question I have had to ask myself on more than one occasion. It's a question I still ask myself on a regular basis.

A Gift from God to Me

I remember sitting in church one Sunday night when I was about twenty-four years old. I had been seriously serving God for awhile, and He had turned my life upside down and inside out. Drunkenness and drugs, which once ruled my life, were now gone. I discovered the joys of reading my Bible, prayer every morning, and if the church doors were open, I was there. God was good, and life was getting better with each passing day. As the pastor was drawing the service to a close that evening, he posed this question: "In what area of your life are you struggling with most and need God's help with right now?"

I watched as others responded to his invitation. Deeply moved, they got out of their seats and walked to the front of the church to pray and lay their struggles down at the altar. I can still remember sitting there and seriously contemplating the pastor's question for several minutes. I thought about how much my life had been turned around since I surrendered myself to Jesus just a few years earlier. I wasn't getting high or drunk anymore, and every other word out of my mouth no longer consisted of four letters.

After a few minutes of contemplation, I distinctly remember coming to the conclusion: *I have nothing wrong in my life at this moment. There isn't anything that I need to lay down at the altar, and I don't need God's help with anything right now.*

Well, just as I began to revel in the thought of my personal progress, Jesus did something that only He can do. He responded to my thoughts and said, *Travis, your biggest problem is the fact that you don't think you have one. What you can't see is that you have way too much pride in your life, and you seem far too content to let it stay there.* Needless to say, that was a humbling experience, and it didn't take long for me to find my own place at the altar repenting from all of the pride that was in my heart. Much of it was religious pride, which I've discovered can be the worst kind; it's a self-righteous pride that convinces you that it's your work rather than the Spirit's work in your life that's producing progress. Religious pride will deceive you into believing that you're righteous because of your prayer life, the number of scriptures you memorized, or how many days a year you've fasted. But none of that makes you righteous or puts you in right standing before God. The only way that happens is by putting your faith in Jesus and His finished work on the cross.

Pride always seems to fly below the radar undetected until one day you wake up and everything that you once held dear is now lost, broken, or dying because of the presence of pride.

In his book *Thirsting for God*, Gary Thomas addressed the issue of pride and the need for us to be open to the insights of others. He noted that:

> "If we want to become like Christ more than anything else, we will welcome insights about our shortcomings. If we supremely value our reputation—that is, if we are motivated by pride— we will resent any implication that we are weak or any revelation that shows our failings...Such an attitude kills any future growth."[15]

Jesus Himself addressed the issue of pride in Luke 14:11 (NASB), declaring, "For everyone who exalts himself will be humbled, and he who humbles himself will be exalted." In that Sunday evening service so many years ago, Jesus gave me a great gift— the gift of showing me the pride that was in my heart and the opportunity to humble myself before Him. I have to be honest with you—initially, this process was pretty painful, and there were many more times like the one I just described where God made it uncomfortably clear that I had unchecked pride in my heart. It's still an ongoing process that won't be completely over until I'm standing face-to-face with Jesus, but the freedom I've received on this side of that loving correction makes all of those healing moments worth it. Every relationship in my life is healthier, and my walk with Jesus is so much more intimate.

The Dirty Dozen

As pride was secretly operating in my life unbeknownst to me, it may be operating in your life unbeknownst to you. While it is very deceptive and difficult to detect, there are some common indicators that pride is present and at work. I call these "The Dirty Dozen."

The twelve warning signs of pride include:

1) **Lack of patience.** The more pride takes hold of your life, the less patient you become. In fact, pride often makes you smug or demanding and hard to work with.
2) **Easily offended.** The seeds of offense can only be sown in the soil of pride. A humble heart deals with and releases offenses quickly. The longer you let offense linger, the more pride is present in your heart.
3) **No longer asking for advice or help.** Pride will cause you to assume you already have all the answers to all of your questions. You don't need help from anyone with anything.
4) **Refusing to admit you're wrong**. Instead of apologizing and admitting when you are wrong, you choose to lose a friend, your job, your ministry, or your marriage.
5) **Afraid of honest feedback.** When you hear constructive criticism that's hard to receive, you become defensive and reject the person who gave it to you.
6) **Developing a "god" complex.** You begin to think you're the only one who could do what you do and the only one who can do it "right."
7) **Justifying the misuse or abuse of others**. You spend more time trying to figure out how people can best benefit your business, ministry, or bank account rather than how your endeavors can best benefit the people you serve.
8) **Times of prayer and Bible reading have stopped.** Prideful people often neglect their relationship with God because

they don't believe they need His help. Or, pride will convince you that your spiritual disciplines make you superior to others or more loved by the Father than other people are.

9) **Talking about yourself incessantly.** Your conversations have become a one-way street where you spend most of the time talking about yourself rather than taking a genuine interest in others.

10) **Dishonoring others.** You privately and publicly criticize and mock others, always assuming you have a better way of doing things.

11) **Doing away with personal development**. You no longer see any reason to read, watch, or listen to material that will help you cultivate your potential spiritually, intellectually, or in your area of gifting to become a more effective leader.

12) **People are avoiding you.** When you call, email, or text, people are not answering or responding because the aroma of pride in your life has become too strong for them to bear.

Do these warning signs sound familiar? They are quite sobering to read through. If you are coming to the realization that you are dealing with a stronghold of pride in your own life, you are probably thinking, *How can I eliminate it? How can I take prideful thoughts captive to the obedience of Christ?* The answer is *humility*. Pride cannot survive in a humble environment. Therefore, we must learn what humility is and how to receive it.

What Humility Is Not

To help define what humility is, I want to state one thing it is *not*. As we have already learned in Romans 12:3, the apostle Paul plainly says to "...not think of yourself more highly than you ought, but rather think of yourself with sober judgment..." (NIV). I'm afraid this verse has been misinterpreted from time to time, and it has ended up taking on a meaning that it was never intended to carry. What you need to understand is that "not thinking of yourself more highly than you ought" doesn't mean that God wants you to think *lowly* of yourself. It just means that you need to keep everything in its proper perspective.

Thinking too little of yourself is *not* what it means to be humble.

Think of it this way. Pride is really nothing more than worship in reverse. It's exalting and magnifying oneself instead of God. Pride is thinking more highly of what *you've* done, while worship is thinking highly of what *God* has done. This includes creating you. You are His masterpiece! You are created in His image and His likeness. Remember, knowing *who* you are and *Whose* you are isn't prideful—it is worship.

A great example of thinking "too highly" of yourself would be what Lucifer did. He became so impressed with himself, he started thinking thoughts like "...I will ascend to heaven; I will raise my throne above the stars of God...I will ascend above the tops of the clouds; I will make myself like the Most High" (Isaiah 14:13-14 NIV). What was the payoff for all of Lucifer's pride? He got kicked out of heaven—pride permanently banned him from the presence of God (see Isaiah 14:15; Ezekiel 28:13-18; Luke 10:18). His name was changed from Lucifer, meaning *star of the morning*, to Satan, meaning *destroyer*. Now, I'm not suggesting that on this side of the cross that Christ will reject you because you're dealing with pride, but I assure you that pride will become a lid on your life.

So what does humility look like? Here are five common characteristics to consider.

Five Attributes of Humble People

HUMBLE PEOPLE DON'T REQUIRE PUBLIC RECOGNITION.

People who struggle with needing public recognition are oftentimes dealing with underlying insecurities and feelings of inferiority. It's not uncommon for these people to go into the local church to try and find a place of service to fill the void within. Far too often their sole purpose is to get public recognition that will temporarily numb the pain of their insecurity. They're trying to get something in God's house to make up for what they aren't getting in their own house. This scenario never turns out well for anybody. It usually ends in some form of offense, leaving the church, and some added emotional baggage for everyone involved.

I am convinced that insecurity is the primary door through which pride is allowed to enter into our hearts. If you go through life constantly needing more public recognition, you will never be satisfied. Your relationships, especially your marriage, and your ability to lead on the job and in ministry will all be strained. Eventually, you'll find yourself isolated and alone. Out of pride, you'll push away everyone that cared enough about you to tell you the truth.

The reality is we all deal with insecurity somewhere in our lives. However, if you're dealing with deep-seated insecurity that you know is detrimentally affecting your ability to move forward in life, then I encourage you to take action. Talk to a pastor, hire a therapist, reach out to a friend. That insecurity will hinder your life as long as you allow it to stay.

Perhaps King David said it best in Psalm 34:3 (NKJV) when he wrote, "Oh, magnify the Lord with me, and let us exalt His name together." We can't start thinking *higher thoughts* until we first realize that we exist to magnify God, not ourselves. It's about exalting *His* Name, not our name.

If your boss or pastor forgets to mention your name in a meeting or email, don't throw a fit. If you don't get the recognition you wanted from your family at home, don't have a meltdown. And if you don't get enough pats on the back for the work you did on a ministry project, don't get offended and disappear from church for three weeks. A humble person doesn't always need recognition because they know that their success isn't based upon being seen. It's based upon making HIM known. I'm not suggesting that recognition is a bad thing because it's not, but if every time you don't get it you become offended, there's a pride problem.

Realize God sees you and is aware of all your efforts. He'll reward you in due time. Therefore, "Whatever may be your task, work at it heartily (from the soul), as [something done] for the Lord and not for men, Knowing [with all certainty] that it is from the Lord [and not from men] that you will receive the inheritance which is your [real] reward. [The One Whom] you are actually serving [is] the Lord Christ..." (Colossians 3:23-24 AMPC).

HUMBLE PEOPLE ADMIT THEIR MISTAKES.

Pride will always tempt us to pass the blame on to another rather than admit our own mistakes. Nothing will cause us to lose credibility with others faster than denying our own faults. On the other hand, humbly admitting our mistakes will serve to build the trust and confidence of others in us.

Remember, the key to receiving grace to handle any situation is humility. Scripture says, "...GOD IS OPPOSED TO THE PROUD, BUT GIVES GRACE TO THE HUMBLE" (1 Peter 5:5 NASB). Therefore, I encourage you to follow God's instructions through the apostle James: "Confess to one another therefore your faults (your slips, your false steps, your offenses, your sins) and pray [also] for one another, that you may be healed and restored..." (James 5:16 AMPC).

HUMBLE PEOPLE ARE GIVERS.

No one exemplifies humble giving better than God the Father. After all, "...God so loved the world, that he gave his only begotten Son..." (John 3:16 KJV). I've heard it said that you can give without loving, but you can't love without giving. Humble people aim to imitate the Father, learning to love and living to give.

This means that you're always on the lookout for ways to invest in the lives of those around you—the incredible people God's called you to do life with and lead. Again, true humility isn't thinking less of yourself, it's simply thinking more of others. So, live to give! As you give, God and others will give back to you, and your life will be blessed in indescribable ways.

HUMBLE PEOPLE THINK OF OTHERS FIRST.

Those pursuing humility recognize that they cannot make it all about themselves and all about God at the same time. Therefore, they put the will of God and the needs of others before their own. With the proud, it is just the opposite.

Author and pastor Gary Thomas said,

> "Proud women and men relate everything back to themselves. They are all but incapable of seeing any situation except for how it affects them. Empathy is something they may read about but will never truly experience."[16]

Regarding those who always think of 'self' first above all others, Thomas also quotes Lorenzo Scupoli saying:

> 'For in everything, whether great or small, they seek their own advantage and like to be preferred before others. They are self-willed and opinionated, blind to their own faults, sharp-sighted when it comes to the faults of others, and they severely condemn the sayings and doings of others.'"[17]

The New Testament is full of verses directing us to put away selfish ambitions and focus on the needs of others. Romans 12:10 (NKJV) instructs us to, "Be kindly affectionate to one another with brotherly love, in honor giving preference to one another." James, the half-brother of Jesus, reveals that sometimes preferring others takes the form of being "...willing to yield" (James 3:17 NKJV) to what is best for them, not us. And in Philippians 2:3-4 (NASB), God tells us through Paul:

> "Do nothing from selfishness or empty conceit, but with humility of mind regard one another as more important than yourselves; do not merely look out for your own personal interests, but also for the interests of others."

What it means to walk in humility can't be made much clearer than this. Being others-minded is a spiritual fruit that each of us as believers must learn how to cultivate. How, you ask? By drawing on the strength and the power of God's Spirit living in us. As we humble ourselves and ask for His help, He will willingly give it, and God will get glory in the process.

HUMBLE PEOPLE ARE SERVANTS.

Overall, if there was one word that describes humility, it is the word *servant*. Jesus said, "...whoever wishes to become great among you shall be your servant" (Matthew 20:26 NASB). Then He said of Himself, "...the Son of Man did not come to be served, but to serve, and to give His life a ransom for many" (Matthew 20:28 NASB).

One of the greatest examples of Jesus' being a Servant took place just hours before He was tortured and crucified. The events are vividly recorded in John's gospel. The Bible says that Jesus "got up from supper, and laid aside His garments; and taking a towel, He girded Himself. Then He poured water into the basin, and began to wash the disciples' feet and to wipe them with the towel with which He was girded" (John 13:4-5 NASB).

In those days, virtually everyone wore sandals as they walked the dusty, dirty roads of Judea and Galilee. Washing feet was the job of the lowest slave in a home. Yet, we see Jesus—Lord of all and equal with God in every way—humbling Himself and taking on the job of the lowest slave in the home.

Scripture goes on to say, "...When He had washed their feet, and taken His garments and reclined at the table again, He said to them, 'Do you know what I have done to you? You call Me Teacher and Lord; and you are right, for so I am. If I then, the Lord and the Teacher, washed your feet, you also ought to wash one another's feet. For I gave you an example that you also should do as I did to you'" (John 13:12-15 NASB).

The greatest picture of humility is the picture of a servant. Think about it: true servants don't require public recognition. They are certainly givers rather than takers, always thinking of the needs of others first, then their own. And if they make mistakes, they don't put the blame on others. They own their actions, apologizing and asking for forgiveness. How can you and I live such a life and model the example Christ set before us? Again, we do it through the strength of His Spirit living in us (see Philippians 4:13).

Humility Is the Key to Promotion

The more I think about it, the more I'm convinced that humility may be one of the most underestimated attributes in life — and in leadership, for that matter. In fact, the Bible reveals that the key to promotion lies in our ability to pursue authentic humility. First Peter 5:6 (NLT) says:

> "So humble yourselves under the mighty power of God, and at the right time he will lift you up in honor."

Isn't that amazing! Despite everything our culture tells us, the key to advancement isn't discovered in self-promotion. It's also not obtained in meeting all the right people, wearing the latest and greatest fashions, having the most prestigious degrees, or amassing the most money. Promotion is found in pursuing and living out authentic humility.

Remember when it came time for God to lead His chosen people out of 400 years of Egyptian captivity? He didn't pick someone with the best résumé or the most experience. He also didn't promote the one with the highest college degrees or most impressive track record. Instead, God chose Moses—a man who had spent the previous forty years of his life serving as a shepherd to his father-in-law's sheep. It was Moses who was chosen for the highest profile leadership position of his time—guiding approximately 1.5 million people into freedom!

Why did God pick Moses? If he was missing many of the attributes that the world recognizes as the winning combination, why was he tapped for the job? God didn't pick Moses because he was the most qualified man on the planet. He was chosen because he was the *humblest* man on the planet. Scripture records:

> "Now the man Moses was very humble, more than any man who was on the face of the earth."
>
> **—Numbers 12:3 (NASB)**

Moses went through times of great adversity, conflict, and waiting before he was promoted. This was all part of the preparation process. I'm convinced that much of the adversity you and I face today is nothing more than God's getting us into position for a promotion—a position of humility.

Speaking from personal experience, I have yet to discover anything more powerful and effective at pushing the pride in our lives out into the open than adversity and conflict. In fact, right now as you are reading this, you may have been wondering why you seem to be going from one battle in your life to the next. The answer may very well be that your struggles are nothing more than God's trying to get you on the spiritual operating table so that He can remove the pride that's quietly destroying your life and keeping you from the future He has planned.

There were times in my life when I experienced great opposition to the dreams that were in my heart. Thinking it was the enemy, I stood against him in prayer. Much to my surprise, I learned that it wasn't the devil that was opposing me—it was God. The reason: pride. In no less than three places, Scripture specifically says that God opposes the proud but gives grace to the humble. The Amplified Bible offers an eye-opening version of one of these verses:

> "...God sets Himself against the proud (the insolent, the overbearing, the disdainful, the presumptuous, the boastful)—[and He opposes, frustrates, and

defeats them], but gives grace (favor, blessing) to the humble."

—1 Peter 5:5 (AMPC)

Friend, if you've been feeling frustrated and defeated for a long time, it may not be the enemy that is opposing you. It may be God. Not because He wants to hurt you, but because He wants to heal you. The more you resist His offer to remove pride, the more adversity He is likely to allow your way. He's not doing it because He is angry with you. He opposes you because He loves you too much to allow pride to remain in your life.

It's Time To Get God Involved

If you really want to tear down the deadly stronghold of pride, you need to get God involved. Ask Him, "Lord, where is pride hiding in my life? What are You trying to show me about myself and about You right now?" Be still and listen. What is He speaking to you?

You could also ask those closest to you if they detect any pride in your life. Yes, it will take courage and humility to ask these questions, but if you're serious about moving your life forward, you have to be willing to receive honest insights from God and those you trust. As my mentor and father in the faith Bishop Mitchell Corder says, "If you want to go where others wish they could go, you have to be willing to do what others are not willing to do." This principle includes self-evaluation and inviting honest feedback about any pride in your life.

Most importantly, realize that humility is not something you can earn or learn on your own. It comes directly from Christ Himself. To have humility is to have the very life of Jesus. In the words of nineteenth-century pastor and author Andrew Murray, humility is "the place of entire dependence on God... The life God bestows is imparted not once for all, but *each moment* continuously, by the unceasing operation of His mighty power."[18]

How can you access this Christlike virtue of all virtues? Murray continues, "It is only by the indwelling of Christ in his divine humility that we become truly humble."[19] Right now Jesus is speaking. Can you hear Him? He's whispering again the invitation offered in Matthew 11:28-29 (NLT):

> "...Come to me, all of you who are weary and carry heavy burdens, and I will give you rest. Take my yoke upon you. Let me teach you, because I am humble and gentle at heart, and you will find rest for your souls."

TAKING IT CAPTIVE:

1 – After reading through this chapter, how has your perception of pride and humility changed?

_____

_____

_____

_____

_____

2 – Take a few minutes to read back over the Dirty Dozen warning signs of pride. Which of these common indicators seem to hit home most? What is God showing you as you read through this list?

_____

_____

_____

_____

_____

3 – Carefully read through the five attributes of humble people. Which of these are you grateful to see operating in your life?

_____

_____

_____

_____

4 – *Humility* is not only the key to promotion, but it also positions you to receive the grace of God. Take some time to look up these treasures from God's Word. What is He showing you in these verses—about humility? About yourself? And about Him?

Psalm 18:27; 25:9; 138:6 • Proverbs 3:34; 15:33; 22:4 • Philippians 2:3-9 • James 4:6-10 • 1 Peter 5:5-6
I believe God is showing me through these passages...

_____

_____

_____

_____

_____

5 – To effectively tear down the deadly stronghold of pride, you need to get God involved. Pause and pray, "Lord, where is pride hiding in my life? What are You trying to show me about myself and about You right now?" Be still and listen. What is He speaking to you?

_____

_____

_____

_____

_____

Chapter 7

"IT'S TOO LATE"

Deadly Thought #4:
The Stronghold of Self-Imposed Limitations

Sarah laughed to herself, saying, "After I have become old,
shall I have pleasure, my lord being old also?"
~ Genesis 18:12 NASB

"The only limit to our realization of tomorrow will
be our doubts of today."[20]

~ Franklin D. Roosevelt

The fourth deadly thought that often keeps people from living out their God-defined purpose is what I call *the stronghold of self-imposed limitations*. Somehow, some way, the enemy convinces people that they are "too this" or "too that." Thoughts like, *I'm too shy, I'm too poor, I'm too young, I'm too old,* or *It's too late* are swallowed again and again until they become a fixed lens through which life is viewed.

The story of Abraham, Sarah, and the birth of Isaac gives us a great example of this. When Abraham was the golden age of ninety-nine, the Lord appeared to him and said, "...I will surely return to you at this time next year; and behold, Sarah your wife will have a son..." (Genesis 18:10 NASB). When Sarah heard this, the

Bible says she "...laughed to herself, saying, 'After I have become old, shall I have pleasure, my lord being old also?'" (v. 12).

Her response reveals that at some point along her journey through life, a stronghold of self-imposed limitations had been established in her mind. Due to great disappointment over her barrenness, she became convinced her best days were behind her. In her mind, she was certain her time for childbearing had passed, and it was too late for her to experience the promises of God.

Have you ever been there? Are you there right now?

Interestingly, the word "laughed" that Sarah used in Genesis 18 is the Hebrew word *tsachaq*. It's a verb that literally means *to mock, toy with, or make sport*. And that's what strongholds will do. They bring you to the point of mocking God's promises for your life. Sarah had bought the lie that the unlimited God, the Creator of the universe, was somehow limited by time.

Can you identify with Sarah? Satan loves to take all of your external circumstances and weaponize them. You can take this to the bank: if there's something the enemy can use against you, he will. He'll harness facts, statistics, and the testimony of others to attack your faith. He'll use your age, lack of experience, or the mistakes you've made to erode your belief in God's Word and convince you it's too late to give birth to your purpose or see God fulfill all of His promises. He'll whisper thoughts to your mind like:

- *It's too late to have a great marriage.*
- *It's too late to be physically, emotionally, or mentally healthy.*
- *It's too late to be happy.*
- *It's too late to go back to school.*
- *It's too late to have a good relationship with your children.*
- *It's too late to get out of debt.*
- *It's too late to be successful.*
- *It's too late to answer the call of God on your life.*
- *It's too late to change your life.*
- *It's too late to start a relationship with God, so why bother trying?*

All of these thoughts are lies. With God, it's *never* too late.

The Moment the Devil Starts Winning

Ever since God's declaration that the Seed of Eve would crush the enemy (see Genesis 3:15), Satan has been greatly afraid of anyone giving birth to someone or something that threatens his existence. Just as he was afraid of the potential within Sarah's womb, he is very much afraid of the potential that God has placed in your (spiritual) womb. That's why he tries so hard to convince you that it's too late to fulfill God's plan and purpose for your life. He knows if he can get you to truly believe *you've missed it,* and *it's too late*, you won't even bother trying. Your purpose would then fall dormant, and you would stop preparing yourself to receive and experience God's promises.

So here's how this works: the moment you stop trying is the moment the devil starts winning. That's the real objective of his attacks on your mind. As with every stronghold, the deadly thought of self-imposed limitations is merely the means to an end. The real win for the enemy is not the establishment of the stronghold itself, but the results it produces.

When the stronghold of self-imposed limitations is present and at work, eventually...

We quit.

We throw in the towel.

We stop trying.

When this stronghold is operating in your life, you begin to limit God to your *own understanding*—confining His work to your time frame, your schedule, your age, your experience, your level of education, and your resources. Leaning on your own under-standing shrinks God's vision for your life down to a size that you think you can manage—something that fits within your own self-imposed limitations. Ultimately, this line of thinking will cause you to take yourself out of the game because you're trying to figure out your life according to how you perceive things.

It's no wonder God penned the powerful words of Proverbs 3:5-6. This timeless truth continues to urge everyone, including you, to "Trust in the Lord with all your heart, and lean not on your own understanding; in all your ways acknowledge Him, and He shall direct your paths" (NKJV). Don't stop trying! Don't quit and leave your destiny undiscovered and your purpose unfulfilled. Trust that in His timing, God will unearth and give birth to the treasure within you.

The Purpose of His Waiting

Undoubtedly, you may be saying to yourself, *Why the long wait? Why did God make Abraham and Sarah wait so long to see the promise fulfilled? As a matter of fact, why is He waiting so long to fulfill His promises in my life?* These are all good questions, and I'd like to address them by examining a family from the town of Bethany who experienced great loss.

Mary, Martha, and their brother Lazarus were all personal friends of Jesus. Not only had they attended many of His camp-meetings, but Jesus had also spent some time with them in their home. It was this same Mary who poured expensive perfume on Jesus' feet and then wiped them with her hair just before He was crucified. And Lazarus was referred to by his sisters as "the one Jesus loved" (see John 11:3). Some have even suggested that Lazarus could have been the mysterious "disciple whom Jesus loved" mentioned repeatedly in John's gospel, and that Lazarus, not John, wrote what we call the Gospel of John. Whatever the case may be, it is clear that the relationship between Jesus and this family was extra special. Indeed, Scripture says, "...Jesus loved Martha and her sister and Lazarus" (John 11:5 NKJV).

However, all of this creates a bit of a paradox for us. Let me explain. When Lazarus became deathly ill, Mary and Martha sent a message to Jesus informing Him of their brother's condition. Instead of coming immediately, the Scriptures record a peculiar response from Jesus. It says:

> "...Although Jesus loved Martha, Mary, and Lazarus, he stayed where he was for the next two days."

—John 11:5-6 (NLT)

So, when Jesus heard that Lazarus, His dear friend, was sick, what did He do? Did He ask Peter to start the camel and point it toward Bethany? No. Did He supernaturally transport Himself back to Lazarus' home? No. Did He speak a word of healing that travelled at the speed of light to where Lazarus was, beating the messenger back to town like He had done with the centurion's servant? No. Scripture tells us that Jesus responded by staying "...where he was for the next two days." In other words, *Jesus waited—on purpose.* And by the time He got to where Lazarus was, Lazarus was already dead. In fact, when Jesus arrived, His friend Lazarus had been in the tomb for four full days.

Grief-stricken by her brother's death, "when Mary arrived and saw Jesus, she fell at his feet and said, 'Lord, if only you had been here, my brother would not have died'" (John 11:32 NLT). In essence, Mary said, "It's too late, Jesus. You waited too long. There's nothing that can be done now."

So why did Jesus wait? If He was so close to Lazarus, why didn't He come to Bethany *before* Lazarus died? He could have prevented his death and saved Mary and Martha the pain of burying their brother and mourning for four days. Jesus revealed His reason for waiting earlier in that chapter, in verses 14 and 15. While speaking to His disciples, He declared, "...Lazarus is dead, and I am glad for your sakes that I was not there, so that you may believe..." (NLT).

As we learned previously, doubt often becomes the lid on our lives and leadership that keeps us from going to the next level. Remember when Jesus went to Nazareth, and He could only do a few miracles there because of their unbelief (doubt)? They had limited the activity of God in their lives because they were held captive by a stronghold of doubt that had poisoned their perception. If we fail to guard ourselves against doubt, the same thing can happen to us.

Personally, I believe Jesus sometimes waits just long enough for our doubts to die. He's not ignoring you—He's preparing you. He hasn't forgotten you—He's transforming you into His image. He's removing the lid of doubt and helping you to truly believe that *the impossible is possible*. Regardless of what you've gone through, it's not too late for Him to come through for you. He's bigger than your circumstances, and He's not bound by space or time. He's tearing down the stronghold of self-imposed limitations.

The *After* Effect

Returning to our story concerning Abraham and Sarah, I want to point out something very important. In order for them to receive the promises of God, they needed to be set free from the roar of the enemy's lie of *It's too late*—especially Sarah. Accordingly, the Lord initiated their journey to freedom by asking a question—a question that when answered would release a revelation of truth.

> "Is anything too difficult for the Lord?" (Genesis 18:14 NASB)

Now, when God asks us a question, it's not because He's looking for answers. He already knows the answers. His purpose is to help *us* find the answers. He's priming our "faith pump" and preparing our minds to receive a revelation of truth that will tear down a stronghold that has held us captive.

I don't know the areas in your life where the enemy has been trying to convince you that it's too late, but more than likely you can relate. Therefore, I want to ask you the same question that God asked Abraham and Sarah—the question that released them from the stronghold of self-imposed limitations:

"Is there anything too difficult for the Lord?"

Ladies and gentlemen, God is no respecter of persons. If He did it for Abraham and Sarah, He will do it for you, too.

Something happened when Sarah heard this question. Somehow, it jolted her to realize that she'd been limiting a limitless God. Due to the barrenness of her womb for years on end, she had allowed her faith for conceiving and giving birth to wane, and at some point she totally stopped believing. Once the Lord confronted this stronghold with His question, He told Abraham and Sarah, "...I will return about this time next year, and Sarah will have a son" (Genesis 18:14 NLT).

Please don't miss this next point! Before God could manifest the miracle through Sarah's womb, He first had to address the limits in her mind. He had to provide her with the truth she needed to tear down the stronghold that convinced her it was too late. Once He did that, she was free to receive the miracle that God had promised.

Personally, I believe that's the primary reason the Lord stopped by Abraham and Sarah's tent. Think about it. When the Lord and the two angels got to the tent, they didn't make small talk with Abraham about how life was going. On the contrary, the Lord cut to the chase, asking for Sarah's whereabouts and telling Abraham that she would give birth to a son about a year later.

Likewise, before God leads you into the next season of your life, He'll start confronting the things that are holding you back. While His dealings may appear as adversity or conflict that makes your life uncomfortable, they're actually a result of His lovingly confronting the strongholds in your life that are keeping you from believing Him. At first, you'll probably be tempted to wonder, *What's happening, God? Why have You made my life so difficult? Please, make it stop!*

But He can't stop! Why? Because it could be that He's preparing you for His promise!

- Believe that your marriage will be healed!
- Believe that your family will be reconciled!
- Believe that your son or daughter will be set free from what has bound them.

Sarah had become a victim of what I call "The *After* Effect." Remember what she said? She rhetorically asked, "*After* I have become old, shall I now have the pleasure of giving my husband a son?" What she didn't realize was that God does some of His best work AFTER!

- *After* Lazarus died, Jesus raised him back to life.
- *After* Job lost everything, God restored to him double what he had.
- *After* the woman had been caught in the act of adultery, Jesus forgave and restored her.
- *After* Jesus had been in the grave for three days, God raised Him up with all power and authority!

Still today, God does some of His best work AFTER! *After* your family comes under attack, He can break through and put the enemy on the run. *After* you don't get the promotion you wanted, He can open a new door of promotion you never knew existed. *After* you receive a bad diagnosis, He can manifest healing in your body, mind, and spirit. *After* you file bankruptcy, He can empower you with head-spinning favor to succeed like you would never have dreamed.

Do you know what happened when the "it's too late" stronghold was destroyed in Sarah's mind? She suddenly found the strength and courage to *try again*.

Try Again!

Now I don't know how to tell you this, but Sarah didn't get pregnant with Isaac the way Mary got pregnant with Jesus. For Sarah to get pregnant, she and Abraham had to...well...*try again*. At the tender ages of 90 and 100 respectively, they had to rediscover the intimacy of their marriage.

That's what happens when strongholds come down. We supernaturally find the courage to believe God again and take corresponding actions based on those beliefs. Abraham and Sarah would never have gotten pregnant and received the promise of God without obediently acting on what they believed God said and trusting His character. Sometimes we think we're waiting for

God to fulfill His promise, but actually it is God Who is waiting for us to act on His promise.

Obedient action places you in position to receive God's promises.

Like Sarah, maybe there's a place in your life where you've tried and tried, but nothing happened. Maybe right now you're saying:

- "I've tried to improve my marriage before, but it didn't work."
- "I've tried to strengthen my family before, but it didn't work."
- "I've tried to get out of debt before, but it didn't work."
- "I've tried to get involved in church before, but I got hurt, and it didn't work."
- "I've tried to move my life forward in many ways, but it just didn't work."

If any of these scenarios sound familiar, I've got good news! You're not alone. Abraham and Sarah had tried and tried and tried to get pregnant for decades, and it didn't work. When it looked like it was too late, the Lord told them, "Try again!"

You say, "But I'm too old." God says, "TRY AGAIN!"

You say, "But it's too late." God says, "TRY AGAIN!"

You say, "But I've made too many mistakes." God says, "TRY AGAIN!"

You say, "But I've been hurt too badly." God says, "TRY AGAIN!"

You may feel like you've already spent your time, wasted your time, or lost too much time to ever see and experience God's promises come to pass in your life. But we serve a God Who knows how to redeem time! God can and will "...restore to you the years that the swarming locust has eaten..." (Joel 2:25 NKJV). After all, we're talking about the same God Who made time stop and the sun stand still (see Joshua 10:12-13). We're speaking of the same Savior Who has an uncanny ability to show up when it looks like it's too late and raise dead things back to life.

In his book *The Grave Robber*, pastor and author Mark Batterson said:

"It's never too late when you turn to the One who can turn back time...It doesn't matter how bad the diagnosis is or how long you've had the handicap. It's never too late to be who you might have been. If you're breathing, it means God's not finished with you yet. You are never past your prime. But if you want a second chance, you need to seek a second opinion—God's opinion."[21]

I don't know what self-imposed limitations are keeping you from pursuing God's will for your life, but *I dare you to try again!* Nothing is too hard for the Lord! It's time to take every ungodly, self-limiting thought captive and make up your mind—by faith— to TRY AGAIN!

It's time to take the "it's too late" thought captive and blow the lid off of your life and leadership. It's time to believe that if God did it for Abraham and Sarah, He can do it for you. And when you're tempted to start thinking that maybe it's too late, just remind yourself that you serve a God Who knows how to create new things out of nothing!

TAKING IT CAPTIVE:

1 – The enemy will use anything he can to try to prevent you from doing the great things God has predetermined for you long ago (see Ephesians 2:10). What self-limiting thoughts have you been hearing and believing that are holding you back from being all God made you to be?

_____

_____

_____

_____

_____

Can you pinpoint a time or event when one of these thoughts first entered your mind? Pause and pray, "Lord, please show me when these thoughts began to take root."

_____

_____

_____

_____

_____

2 – Is there a dream or promise God has placed in you? If so, take time to briefly describe it.

_____

_____

_____

3 – *Obedient action* activates God's promises. For Abraham and Sarah, they needed to rediscover the intimacy of their marriage when all hope seemed gone. What corresponding actions do you feel the Lord is asking you to take at this time?

_____

_____

_____

_____

_____

4 – With God, *it is never too late* to see His promises become reality in your life. Take some time to meditate on these verses. Jot down what God is showing you, and write out at least two that you find most encouraging.

Matthew 19:26 • Luke 1:37 • 2 Corinthians 9:8 • Philippians 4:13 • Ephesians 3:20
I believe God is showing me through these passages...

_____

_____

_____

_____

_____

The verses that encourage me most are...

_____

_____

_____

_____

_____

Chapter 8

"I CAN'T"

DEADLY THOUGHT #5: THE STRONGHOLD OF FEAR

For God has not given us a spirit of fear,
but of power and of love and of a sound mind.
~ 2 Timothy 1:7 (NKJV)

"The way you see yourself will determine the kind
of demands you place on yourself."[22]

~ Bishop T.D. Jakes

The fifth deadly thought is *I Can't*, and it's rooted in the stronghold of fear. Fear enters our lives in many different ways. There's the fear of failure, fear of defeat, fear of the future, fear of what others think, and the fear of embarrassment or rejection, to name a few. There is also a fear that those around us will somehow see the brokenness inside of us if we let them get too close. Regardless of its form, fear poisons the perception we have of ourselves, causing us to view adversity through a lens of defeat. This keeps us from fighting for God's promises by convincing us, before we even try, that the fight could never be won. Which brings us to one of the most damaging byproducts of fear—the *Grasshopper Syndrome*.

The Grasshopper Syndrome

The Grasshopper Syndrome is a condition that causes you to view yourself as someone that's "too" something—too small, too weak, too inexperienced, too young, too old, too poor, or too dysfunctional to ever defeat the giants that stand between you and your destiny. It's a mindset rooted in fear that causes your obstacles to look bigger and bigger while making God seem smaller and smaller. One of the most dangerous side effects of the Grasshopper Syndrome is that it doesn't just affect the way you see yourself. It affects the way you think others see you, as well.

In Numbers 13, we see the Israelites had a major run-in with the stronghold of fear. It was right around the same time we all do— right before we're about to step into the promises of God. Take a look at what happened:

> "But the men who had gone up with him said, 'We are not able to go up against the people, for they are too strong for us.' So they gave out to the sons of Israel a bad report of the land which they had spied out, saying, 'The land through which we have gone, in spying it out, is a land that devours its inhabitants; and all the people whom we saw in it are men of great size. There also we saw the Nephilim (the sons of Anak are part of the Nephilim); and *we became like grasshoppers in our own sight, and so we were in their sight.*'"
>
> **—Numbers 13:31-33 (NASB)**

As a result of the fall, we as human beings are bent toward the negative. When we look into the mirror, we tend to see and focus on all of our weaknesses and imperfections. We concentrate on the stuff we don't like about ourselves and wish we could change. Consequently, we're secretly scared to death that the people around us can see our weaknesses and imperfections the same way we do.

Have you ever been around somebody who complained about the way they looked and you thought, *What in the world is she talking about? She looks great!* Well, that's probably what other people are thinking every time you say negative things about yourself. The reason we complain out loud about ourselves is that we assume that what we see and don't like about ourselves is also what others see and don't like about us. That's the Grasshopper Syndrome. It is a mindset rooted in fear with the prevailing thought of *I Can't*.

This deadly mindset takes hold of our life when we spend too much of our time and energy focusing on the obstacles in front of us and/or the brokenness within us rather than on our God Who is for us. The longer we soak in the idea of how big our problems are or how flawed we think we are, the more magnified those flaws and problems become. Before we know it, we start to assume that "others" see us the same way we see ourselves, just like ten of the twelve spies saw themselves in Numbers 13.

Magnify and Minimize

Our minds tend to work like a telescope or pair of binoculars. That is, what we focus our attention on is magnified in our mind, appearing much larger than it actually is. Oftentimes, Satan will tempt you to take your focus off God and point your telescope or binoculars (your mind) at your problems, flaws, and failures. Once you've taken the bait and started to focus on the negative, your troubles and weaknesses become magnified. What happens to your view of God? By default, and with the help of the enemy, He is minimized in your sight, seeming smaller, weaker, or less capable of keeping His promises to you.

Have you ever looked through a telescope or a pair of binoculars *backwards*? It makes everything look much smaller and much further away than it really is. In times of trial and temptation, the enemy takes the binoculars or telescope (your mental perception), and he flips it around so that as you look at God, He seems small or too far away to help. If you allow him, Satan will keep bouncing your perception of things back and forth, causing you to see your situations and your weaknesses as *too big* to conquer and your God as *too small* to enable you to win. Hence, the deadly thought of *I Can't* takes root, and the enemy has the advantage.

The *I Can't* mentality is what kept eleven disciples in the boat while Peter walked on the water. It's why abuse victims keep hooking up with abusers and why qualified people stay in the same dead end jobs. It's not because they can't do any better but because they refuse to think better about who they are and who God created them to be. The *I Can't* mentality is the reason churches aren't planted, marriage vows are aborted, books are never written, and businesses never begin. The spirit of fear is at work, fueling the fire of the Grasshopper Syndrome. If this attack is tolerated, you'll eventually become so discouraged that you'll simply give up on your marriage, family, ministry, and even life itself because it all seems so hopeless.

The Way You See You

The Israelites didn't realize how lowly they thought of themselves until they were faced with adversity. What's true for them is often true for us. Seeing and understanding their reaction to the challenges before them offers us a biopsy of their thought life, helping us understand what's going on inside of us. Look carefully at how they saw themselves:

> "There also we saw the Nephilim (giants); and we became like grasshoppers in our own sight, and so we were in their sight."
>
> —Numbers 13:33 (NASB)

After reading that verse, I am left with a question: How in the world did the Israelites know what the giants were thinking? Did they stand in the middle of the street with clipboards asking them, "Excuse me... We're thinking about attacking your city and taking your land, but there's something we need to settle first.

We think that we look like grasshoppers in your sight. What do you think about us?" Of course they didn't do that! The problem wasn't with the giants in front of them. The real issue was with the stronghold of fear inside of them—that never-ending voice of doom that kept saying, *You can't do this! You're too small, too inexperienced, and too weak to win.*

The more they thought of their enemies, the less they thought of themselves. The reality is that the adversity in front of them never got any bigger, and the promises of God never got any smaller. But they were infected with the Grasshopper Syndrome, and it didn't just affect the way they thought about themselves. They actually started to project their thoughts onto those around them, saying, "We look like grasshoppers in our own sight, and that's what they think of us, too."

I personally believe God was trying to use the giants to show the Israelites just how low they had begun to think of both their God and themselves. I think God was using the adversity in front of them to confront the insecurity and fear inside of them. Had they dealt with their low thinking head-on, and by faith decided to focus on the promises of God rather than the size of their enemies and what they assumed they were thinking about them, they would have stepped directly into God's promises and their purpose. Instead, their low thinking caused them to forfeit their destiny, living the remaining forty years of their existence wandering around the wilderness until they died.

Satan's objective is always to steal, kill, and destroy anything and everything he can, including your faith (see John 10:10). Faith is the ability to confidently believe you have what you cannot see or touch. Interestingly, when it comes to the enemy's attempts to destroy you with fear, his strategy is not always to eliminate your faith, but to hijack it and use it as a weapon against you. That is, a spirit of fear will often cause you to have more faith in the enemy and the obstacles he's erected than in the all-powerful, all-knowing God.

To help you more accurately detect if there is a stronghold of fear in your life, let's take a look at some of the most common symptoms of fear and see what God's Word says in response to them.

Five Symptoms of Fear and God's Antidote
#1—DECISION PARALYSIS
"I CAN'T afford to make the wrong decision."

Fear will cause you to suffer from what I call "decidophobia"—the fear of making decisions. Afraid that you will miss out on something better, that you'll make the wrong decision, or that you'll fail altogether, you become paralyzed from making any decision at all. *I can't afford to make a mistake*, you'll tell yourself. *I can't take the risk of doing this wrong.*

Every time I see a dead squirrel or possum in the middle of the road, I'm reminded of the dangers of indecision. The only thing more dangerous than making the wrong decision is making no decision at all. Think about it. Even when you make the wrong decision, it can become a learning opportunity from which you can grow. But if you allow the stronghold of fear and the thought of *I Can't* to convince you to make no decision at all, you lose opportunities to make progress toward your purpose.

The good news is that God has promised to guide you in every decision. In Psalm 32:8 (NASB) He says, "I will instruct you and teach you in the way which you should go; I will counsel you with My eye upon you." In Isaiah 30:21 (NKJV) He says, "Your ears shall hear a word behind you, saying, 'This is the way, walk in it.'" And in Psalm 25, which is filled with promises of God's divine direction, He says, "Who are those who fear the Lord? He will show them the path they should choose" (v. 12 NLT).

Again and again, God tells us not to be afraid and to trust Him for His guidance. All He wants and requires from us is a humble heart that is willing to ask for His direction. This probably couldn't be any clearer than His words through James: "If you do not have wisdom, ask God for it. He is always ready to give it to you and will never say you are wrong for asking" (James 1:5 NLT). So don't be afraid to make a decision. Humble yourself in prayer, and ask Him for direction. He will show you what to do. And when you do make a mistake or choose the wrong direction, He knows how to help you get back on track and redeem the mistake for your good.

#2–Relational Isolation
"I CAN'T open myself up to be hurt again."

Another tactic of fear is to get us to pull away and isolate ourselves from others. When we've been hurt, our natural response is to push people away and refuse to let them in—many times without even realizing it. In order to keep us from being hurt again, a stronghold of fear will cause us to unknowingly act and react in ways that sabotage our relationships.

The problem is that isolation comes before devastation. It's an age-old tactic. Satan wants to get you off by yourself and keep you fighting the battle of trying to protect yourself–by yourself. He knows that as long as you're fighting this battle alone in the dark, you're fighting on his turf, and as the prince of darkness, he has a much better chance of holding you back from God's best.

When I was a kid growing up in church, we used to sing an old song that said, "He's all I need, all I need. Jesus is all I need." I understand the spiritual intent of the song, but at face value, the words are misleading. God created us to need relationships. Galatians 6:2 tells us that the way to fulfill the law of Christ is to "Bear one another's burdens..." (NASB). In the Gospels, when Jesus sent out His disciples, He sent them out in groups of two. And let's also not forget that in the beginning, when God first created man, He said, "It is not good for the man to be alone..." (Genesis 2:18 NIV).

Clearly, the enemy has worked hard at convincing us that needing others in our lives is a sign of weakness. He wants us to think that in order to be a hero, we have to adopt the motto "I don't need anybody!" The truth is, however, we *do* need each other.

Just as the enemy used people to hurt you, God wants to work through people to heal you. In fact, some of the very people you're trying to keep out of your life may be the very ones God wants to use to heal your brokenness. Scripture says if we confess our sins to God, we'll be forgiven (see 1 John 1:9). But according to James 5:16, it's not until we learn to confess our sins to each other that we're healed. Not that it's sinful to be broken, because it's not, but there's a principle locked up in this verse that points to our need for someone to talk to and process our pain with if we're going to heal. There are a lot of forgiven people in church today who have never been healed from relational wounds. They talk to God but reject relationships with people, so they continue to struggle with unnecessary pain that's keeping them from the peace and joy that Jesus promised them.

You were made for relationship—you need people in your life. I believe Ecclesiastes 4:9-10 (NASB), probably says it best:

> "Two are better than one because they have a good return for their labor. For if either of them falls, the one will lift up his companion. But woe to the one who falls when there is not another to lift him up."

#3—RETREATING IN DEFEAT
"I CAN'T win."

Fear also comes in the thought of *I Can't win*. Afraid of failing, we develop a pattern of retreating. Instead of embracing opportunities to do something fresh and new, we run from them. In an attitude of defeat, we begin to say things like, "That's too big for me...someone like me could never do that. I don't have enough experience. I don't know the right people."

If these phrases sound eerily familiar, it might be because the enemy has been at work. Like the Israelites, he has convinced you to see yourself as a *grasshopper*. Consequently, you'll only try things that you've tried before. You'll only apply for grasshopper jobs. If you're single, you'll only go on grasshopper dates. Or you'll only pursue a grasshopper education because that's how you see yourself—as a grasshopper.

Remember the story of David and Goliath? There was something about David that separated him from the rest of the Israelite army. It was his perspective. When David saw Goliath, he didn't see a giant. He saw an *opportunity*. No, he didn't have previous experience defeating giants, and no, he didn't own superior weaponry with which to fight. Yet, he wasn't afraid to entrust himself to God and try something he had never tried before. He chose to see himself as God saw him, and he refused to let fear keep him from his God-given destiny.

Be sure of this: God did not call you to retreat—He created you to overcome. In Christ, you are a winner! "What then shall we say to these things? If God is for us, who can be against us?" (Romans 8:31 NKJV) David knew that God was for him, and you need to know it, believe it, and declare it, too. Romans 8:11 (NKJV) says, "...The Spirit of Him who raised Jesus from the dead dwells in you...," and in verse 37 of the same chapter God declares, "...In all these things we are more than conquerors through Him who loved us" (NKJV).

Like David, you have the ability to take God-ordained risks and believe that you are going to succeed. Stop retreating, and start defeating the spirit of fear trying to hold you back. Stretch your faith and move forward out of your comfort zone. Make these words of the apostle Paul your declaration: "...Thanks be to God, who always leads us in triumph in Christ..." (2 Corinthians 2:14 NKJV).

#4–Going in Circles
"I CAN'T move forward."

A spirit of fear will not only cause you to ditch relationships, retreat in defeat, and avoid making decisions. It will also make you wander around in circles, keeping you from moving forward in the good things God has planned. Again, think about the Israelites trying to enter the Promised Land. They put more faith in the lies that Satan fed them than in the power of God to promote them. They believed the enemy was bigger and more powerful than the God Who had promised them victory. They saw themselves as grasshoppers and believed their enemies saw them that way too. As a result, they spent the rest of their lives literally going in circles, wandering in the desert, unable to move forward.

Refusing to deal with the stronghold of fear will result in many a wasted year. We'll find ourselves living in a dried up marriage, dried up ministry, or dried up family. Over and over, we'll keep repeating the same destructive cycles. That's why we can't afford to allow this kind of low thinking to stick around in our lives.

Sometimes being busy is the same thing as going in circles. Busyness can trick us into feeling like we're being productive— aka moving forward—when in reality, we're just going in circles trying to avoid the fact that we're stuck in one place. Please hear me. Until your frustration with your progress becomes greater than your fear of the process, you'll never step into your God-given purpose.

The enemy is not worried about your being busy. In fact, if you'll allow him, he will keep you on the treadmill of religious performance, making you believe that the only way to be used by God is to work hard enough to please God rather than trust in the finished work of Jesus on the cross. He'll keep you juggling multiple projects and problems until he thoroughly exhausts you. He'll try to keep you busy by convincing you that

- for God to love you, you have to impress Him with your religious performance.
- your identity is tied to your activity, so stay busy if you want to be valuable.
- if your project fails, you're a failure.
- anything less than perfection in your marriage, ministry, job or family is unacceptable and diminishes your worth.

What's the alternative to being constantly busy but accomplishing nothing? The answer is trusting in the finished work of Jesus and choosing to rest in God's promises. Scripture says to "Trust in the Lord with all your heart and do not lean on your own understanding. In all your ways acknowledge Him, and He will make your paths straight" (Proverbs 3:5-6 NASB). While a lack of trust in God will keep us wandering in circles like the Israelites, trusting in God will move us forward into the reality of the promises He's made concerning our life and future. Receiving God's love, favor, forgiveness and purpose for your life isn't about what you're able to do, but what Jesus already accomplished on the cross. All that's left for you to do is receive all the good things your heavenly Father has for you; this is what it means to stop striving to make something happen and simply choosing to believe God and enter His rest. Chapter 4 of Hebrews says it like this:

> "For we who have believed enter that rest... For the one who has entered His rest has himself also rested from his works, as God did from His. Therefore let us be diligent to enter that rest, so that no one will fall, through following the same example of disobedience."
>
> —Hebrews 4:3, 10-11 (NASB)

#5—IMPOSING YOUR FEARS ON OTHERS
Moving from "I CAN'T" to "WE CAN'T."

Left unchecked, fear will eventually expand its influence in your life and attempt to reach into the lives of others close to you. It will cause you to move from saying "I can't" to "We can't." Your negative, fearful perspective will turn you into a dispenser of fear, and you will begin imposing your thinking on the people closest to you—many times unknowingly. For example, fear caused ten of the twelve spies to look at life through the lens of negativity. They totally ignored the miraculous signs and wonders God had performed as He delivered them from Egyptian bondage. Instead of trusting His mighty acts as proof that He would make good on His promise to defeat their enemies and bring them into the Promised Land, they spread a negative report among the people, telling them that the land "devours its inhabitants" (Numbers 13:32).

But wait a minute. What happened to the land that was flowing with milk and honey that they had just seen? What about the huge cluster of grapes that was so big it took two men to carry back the sample that they cut from the vine? (See Numbers 13:23.) Fear had poisoned their perception, causing them to dismiss the evidence of God's promises and take on the Grasshopper Syndrome. And they said, "We can't do this!"

Are you tired of the deadly *I Can't* thought constantly telling you what you can and can't do? Are you ready to pull down the stronghold of fear? Then here's what you need to do.

Worship Works Wonders!

Begin to WORSHIP! Yes, I said worship. Why? Because when it comes to fighting fear, worship is an incredibly powerful weapon. Let me explain.

When you worship, you're turning your attention to the God Who loves you rather than to the problems around you, and your problems start looking smaller and smaller as your God starts looking bigger and bigger. The more we sing about or meditate on God's love, grace, and goodness, the more our minds are renewed and the more we give ourselves permission to receive all the good things our Father has for us. One of the most effective ways to restore our joy and protect our peace is to turn our attention to the Lord and simply worship. It purifies our perception and restores a kingdom perspective. The Bible says that God is love. It's not just something He does—it's Who He is (see 1 John 4:8). The more we experience His love, the greater our understanding of His love grows, and fear's stronghold on our hearts and minds is broken.

> "There is no fear in love; but *perfect love casts out fear...*"
>
> —1 John 4:18 (NASB)

I have learned that it's very difficult to worship and worry at the same time. Worry is just another manifestation of fear, along with anxiety, doubt, and dread. It's nearly impossible for worship and worry to occupy the same space in your heart and mind simultaneously.

David is one of the most well-known worshipers in Scripture. He is credited for writing about 76 of the 150 Psalms. It was David who wrote:

> "I will bless the Lord at all times; His praise shall continually be in my mouth."

> —Psalm 34:1 NKJV

Indeed, David understood the value of worship when it came to cultivating his love relationship with God. Maybe that's why he could also fearlessly write, "Yea, though I walk through the valley of the shadow of death, I will fear no evil..." (Psalm 23:4 NKJV) and, "I am not afraid of ten thousand enemies who surround me on every side" (Psalm 3:6 NLT). Fear could never keep its grip on David because he never stopped worshiping and keeping his focus on God. Worship eradicates fear and magnifies the reality of God's presence in your life. To be clear, we don't worship to get God's presence in our lives, we worship because we already have it! Once you put your faith in Jesus, God promises in Deuteronomy 31:6 (NIV) that He "...will never leave you nor forsake you." And in Matthew 28:20 (NIV), Jesus said, "...I am with you always, to the very end of the age." This is often where so many who have put their faith in Jesus get tripped up. They think that they need to worship in order to receive something from God. That's simply not true. On this side of the cross, the reason we worship is not to get something from God, but because in Christ, God's already provided everything we need! We don't worship because we have to, we worship because we get to.

If you're serious about pulling down the stronghold of fear, then shut the door, turn on your favorite worship music, lift your hands and start to worship. Can't sing? No problem. God doesn't need you to sound good in your ears for it to sound good to Him. He is your Father, and you are His child. He loves you, He won't reject you, and He wants to commune with you. Fear doesn't stand a chance against your worship.

Pray About Everything

As we close this chapter, I want to remind you of one more weapon in the arsenal in your fight against fear — *prayer*. Along with worship, remember to pray about everything. Through the apostle Paul, God gives us a powerful prescription for the infection of fear. He says:

> "Don't worry about anything; instead, *pray about everything*. Tell God what you need, and thank him for all he has done. If you do this, you will experience God's peace, which is far more wonderful than the human mind can understand. His peace will guard your hearts and minds as you live in Christ Jesus."

—Philippians 4:6-7 (NLT)

Friend, God is **for** you, not against you. He is your Guardian God of Psalm 121. He has given His angels a specific assignment to watch over you in all your ways and through all your days (see Psalm 91). Whenever you find yourself afraid, cry out to Him! David said, "I sought the Lord, and he answered me; he delivered me from all my fears. This poor man called, and the Lord heard him; he saved him out of all his troubles" (Psalm 34:4, 6 NIV). God is no respecter of persons. What He did for David and what He has done for countless others, He will do for you!

TAKING IT CAPTIVE:

1 – The deadly thought of *I Can't* can be paralyzing. Stop and think: *What are the **top three** areas of my life where I am knowingly (or unknowingly) thinking* I Can't *do something?* These are areas in which you know you need to move forward, but you are afraid.

1. _____

2. _____

3. _____

Now pause and pray, "Lord, please show me the specific thought(s) of fear or worry that I have accepted that are holding me back. Tell me any specific action I need to take to defeat it."

_____

_____

_____

_____

_____

2 – The Israelites saw themselves as grasshoppers and believed their enemies saw them the same way. Be honest, how would you describe *the way you see yourself* (in general on a daily basis)?

_____

_____

_____

_____

_____

Again, be honest, and describe how you think *others see you* (friends and family, as well as those you consider enemies).

_____

_____

_____

_____

_____

3 – How do you think *God sees you*? Take a moment and jot down your honest feelings. Then check out these verses revealing the truth about how He sees you. What is He showing you?

2 Corinthians 5:17, 21 • 1 John 3:1-2 • Psalm 139:13-14, 17-18 • Deuteronomy 7:6 • 1 Peter 2:9-10

_____

_____

_____

_____

I believe God is showing me through these passages...

_____

_____

_____

_____

_____

4 – Instead of your thinking _I Can't_, God wants you to think and believe _I Can_. While you are power*less* on your own, you are pow-er*ful* in Him. Take some time to meditate on these promises from His Word to you. How do they strengthen and encourage you in your walk with Him?

Isaiah 40:28-31; 41:10-13 • Philippians 4:13 • Luke 10:19 • Psalm 27:1-6; 34:4-8 • Hebrews 13:5-6

These promises from God encourage me...

_____

_____

_____

_____

The verses that encourage me most are...

_____

_____

_____

_____

Chapter 9

"FORGIVENESS IS OPTIONAL"

DEADLY THOUGHT #6: THE STRONGHOLD OF UNFORGIVENESS

Good sense and discretion make a man slow to anger,
And it is his honor and glory to overlook a transgression or an
offense [without seeking revenge and harboring resentment].
~ Proverbs 19:11(AMP)

"When you forgive, you in no way change the past—
but you sure do change the future."[23]

~ Bernard Meltzer

The sixth deadly thought doesn't discriminate and knows no boundaries. It pays no attention to race, age, gender, or level of education. Its host can be a son or daughter, mother or father, rich or poor, sinner or saint and infects those both within and without the Church. It is the deceptive mindset that *Forgiveness Is Optional* and that unforgiveness holds no consequences. It's rooted in the stronghold of unforgiveness, also known as offense.

Unforgiveness is a deadly poison that often slips suddenly into the recesses of our heart cloaked in the guise of self-protection. Like an expensive street drug, it offers a temporary escape from our current reality, all the while keeping its destructive nature out of sight. It promises great things—power, protection, and justice—but never delivers. It finds us full but leaves us empty.

If we're honest, we'll admit that we have all done something to someone at some time that was offensive—most of the time unintentionally. Nevertheless, we hurt them by what we did or said. To make amends, we apologized and asked for their forgiveness. When they accepted our apology and extended their forgiveness, we were filled with gratefulness and appreciation. It was as if a load had been lifted off us, and we had peace within. But what if the tables were turned? What if you were the one on the receiving end of offense? Do you ever have the right to hold onto a person's offense and not forgive?

The Answer Is Clear

In Matthew 18:21, Peter asked Jesus, "Lord, how often shall my brother sin against me and I forgive him? Up to seven times?" In verse 22 Jesus responded, "I do not say to you, up to seven times, but up to seventy times seven"(NASB). Then to teach us how important forgiveness is Jesus tells us the parable of the unforgiving servant:

> "Therefore, the Kingdom of Heaven can be compared to a king who decided to bring his accounts up to date with servants who had borrowed money from him. In the process, one of his debtors was brought in who owed him millions of dollars. He couldn't pay, so his master ordered that he be sold—along with his wife, his children, and everything he owned—to pay the debt.

> "But the man fell down before his master and begged him, 'Please, be patient with me, and I will pay it all.' Then his master was filled with pity for him, and he released him and forgave his debt.

"But when the man left the king, he went to a fellow servant who owed him a few thousand dollars. He grabbed him by the throat and demanded instant payment.

"His fellow servant fell down before him and begged for a little more time. 'Be patient with me, and I will pay it,' he pleaded. But his creditor wouldn't wait. He had the man arrested and put in prison until the debt could be paid in full.

"When some of the other servants saw this, they were very upset. They went to the king and told him everything that had happened. Then the king called in the man he had forgiven and said, 'You evil servant! I forgave you that tremendous debt because you pleaded with me. Shouldn't you have mercy on your fellow servant, just as I had mercy on you?' Then the angry king sent the man to prison to be tortured until he had paid his entire debt.

—Matthew 18:23-34 (NLT)

This parable presents us with a no-nonsense question: who are we, who have received so much, to withhold so little? Our sin created such a great debt that God had to send His Son to pay the price. When you stop to consider the brutal torture endured by our Savior, who are we to try to hold someone hostage for the pain they've caused us?

Some people erroneously think that if they refuse to forgive someone who's hurt them, they're somehow hurting them back. But the exact opposite is true. Refusing to forgive someone is like drinking poison and then wishing the other person would die. Just like the unforgiving servant in Matthew 18, when we buy the lie that *Forgiveness Is Optional*, the one being tortured is us.

Even among believers, who are recipients of God's grace and claim loyalty to Jesus, there seems to be a growing temptation to avoid dealing with unforgiveness. I guess this shouldn't surprise us. Jesus warned that the love of many would grow cold, and that Satan would deceive even the very elect (see Matthew 24:10-12, 24). I've met and counseled with good church-going people who refused to forgive someone who hurt them. When I explained the dangers of their decision not to forgive, they responded by saying, "But you don't know what they did to me! You just don't understand how badly they've hurt me." Even after I walked them through the scriptures dealing with God's call to forgive, they somehow thought those truths didn't apply to their situation. They believed they were the exception to the rule.

Listen, I get it. It is painful to be hurt, and nobody wants to be hurt again. But when it comes to pain, the most dangerous thing in life isn't getting hurt—it's staying hurt. Hurt people end up hurting people. Likewise, rejected people end up rejecting people, and wounded people end up wounding people. The cycle is vicious. Unless we make an active choice to forgive and release the person who has offended us, the stronghold of unforgiveness will become firmly established in our mind, preventing us from building healthy relationships, giving and receiving love, and pursuing our God-given purpose. Holding onto offense and refusing to forgive will eventually produce bitter roots in our hearts. None of us is immune to the consequences of harboring unforgiveness.

Bitter Roots

Now, you may ask, "How is bitterness different from unforgiveness?" The difference has to do with time. When someone offends us by something they have said or done, we are hurt. The offense is fresh, and we have a choice to bring it to God and receive His grace to forgive the person, or we can hold onto the offense and not forgive. The longer we hold onto an offense, the more deeply rooted unforgiveness becomes. Over time, unforgiveness that has been festering in our hearts turns into a root of bitterness.

Through the writer of Hebrews, God instructs us to:

> "Pursue peace with all people...lest any *root of bitterness* springing up cause trouble, and by this many become defiled."

> **—Hebrews 12:14-15 (NKJV)**

Bitter roots produce bitter fruit. Holding onto unforgiveness somewhere in your life will produce bitterness in every part of your life. And notice that Hebrews 12 doesn't say that a bitter root in your life only impacts you. It says that because of the bitterness in one life, "...MANY become defiled." You can't compartmentalize bitterness. It doesn't just poison your life; it poisons the lives of everyone close to you. If not dealt with, it eventually grows out of control and starts spilling into other areas of your life that were previously healthy—especially other relationships. Like a python snake, a bitter root will slowly wrap itself around your heart and choke the love out of every part of your life. It's often not until something of great value in your life has died that you start to realize something is dangerously wrong.

Refusing to forgive will eventually produce some dangerous consequences:

- Refusing to forgive one's parents for something they did years ago allows a root of bitterness to grow and eventually choke the love out of that person's relationship with their own children.
- Refusing to forgive an ex-spouse for having an affair allows a root of bitterness to grow and eventually choke the love and intimacy out of that person's current marriage.
- Refusing to forgive people who hurt us at our last church allows a root of bitterness to grow, eventually choking the love and joy out of our experiences at our new church.

Again, bitter roots produce bitter fruit. The longer we choose not to forgive, the more painful and more numerous the side effects will become. Frustration, irritation, aggravation, lack of joy, the constant presence of anger, and a lack of peace are just a few of the mounting miseries that accompany roots of bitterness.

For the remainder of this chapter, I want to examine six symptoms of a bitter root and what we need to do to get free from it. As you read, see if you can recognize any of these operating in your own life. If you do, you may have some unresolved unforgiveness in your heart that, with the help of Jesus, you need to evict.

Six Symptoms of a Bitter Root

Symptom 1: THE LOOK ON YOUR FACE

To those who know you best, the look on your face will always tell the story of your heart. It's true for all of us. Isaiah 3:9 (NASB) says, "The expression of their faces bears witness against them..." You might be able to hide unforgiveness for a little while, but as time wears on, all of that extra energy you're using to cover up your bitterness will expire and give way to emotional fatigue. Your true feelings will start leaking out. People you live and work with will begin to notice that something is off just by looking at you. You know that if you make eye contact with them, they'll be able to tell that something is wrong. So you avoid interacting with them at all costs, thus avoiding the relational accountability that could help you get free. Eventually, the hurt you've kept hidden in your heart will begin to spill out through your words and attitude.

In the book of Genesis, it says when Cain became bitterly jealous of his brother Abel, he "...was very angry, and his face was downcast. Then the Lord said to Cain, 'Why are you angry? Why is your face downcast? If you do what is right, will you not be accepted? But if you do not do what is right, sin is crouching at your door; it desires to have you, but you must rule over it'" (Genesis 4:5-7 NIV).

When God addressed Cain, He pointed to his countenance (the look on his face) as evidence that something was off in his heart. Our facial expression serves as a sort of emotional thermometer that lets us know when we or someone around us is heading for trouble. Out of love, God addressed Cain's anger that was a warning sign of the bitterness in his heart. He was giving Cain the opportunity to deal with his offense with his brother before he and his whole family would be affected by the bitter root.

I believe that is what God is doing for those reading this book, possibly even you. What does your face say about what's in your heart? Now is the time to surrender any bitterness before it grows out of control and something much more dangerous takes place down the road.

Symptom 2: IMPATIENCE

The longer a bitter root is present, the less patience you'll have. Your fuse will get shorter and shorter, and your temper will grow hotter and hotter. You'll find yourself losing your peace over things that are really insignificant. Things that never used to bother you will really begin irritating you. You'll go off on the person handing you your French fries through the drive-thru window because they gave you a medium instead of the large you ordered. Without rhyme or reason, the slightest inconvenience will begin to emotionally flip your switch and set off a totally irrational response. Sitting in traffic, slow internet service, the newspaper thrown in the bushes, you name it. Everything will turn personal and be perceived as an intentional act of disrespect toward you.

You'll start turning molehills into mountains, and everyone around you will begin to act as though they were walking on eggshells for fear of the possible fallout that could come from saying the wrong thing the wrong way. You'll have no patience for those who don't see things your way, move at your pace, or meet your expectations. Your family will begin making excuses not to be around you. Your spouse will start working overtime and taking extra hours at work in order to avoid the turmoil of being around you. The reason: unforgiveness is squeezing the love out of your heart.

The remedy for this manifestation of impatience is to address the bitter root of unforgiveness in your heart. When you admit you're hurt and submit your hurt to the Lord, He will release

His peace and a fresh outlook on life. This is confirmed in Acts 3:19 (NIV):

> "Repent, then, and turn to God, so that your sins may be wiped out, that times of refreshing may come from the Lord."

Symptom 3: INDIFFERENCE

The third common symptom of a bitter root is indifference. That is, you become cold, less compassionate, and less merciful toward others. As love is choked out of your heart, your tolerance for the shortcomings of others goes out the window. This soon gives way to cutting off relationships with those you deem no longer add to your life. You begin avoiding their phone calls, as well as ignoring their text messages and emails. If you know that a person or people are going to be at a certain place or event, you avoid going there.

Ironically, while the faults and failures of others become more and more glaring, you become blind to your own. People who were once considered good friends start looking like enemies in your mind. *I don't have time for them*, you tell yourself. *We just don't see eye to eye*. Sound familiar? If so, it could be a warning sign that a bitter root is growing and choking out the fruit of humility that comes from Christ.

Symptom 4: FEAR

A growing root of bitterness can also open the door to other destructive elements in your life—chief among them is fear. The enemy will take full advantage of your condition and bring fear in all its forms against you. He will cause you to chronically worry about things that will never happen. News reports will keep you awake at night for hours. Even if you manage to get some sleep, you'll find it impossible to actually rest. You'll wake up day after day feeling exhausted because unforgiveness has produced fear that causes you to worry and have anxiety about everything.

Maybe worst of all, fear will keep you from moving forward, making decisions, and letting people into your life. A growing distrust and suspicion will begin to fence you in, blockading you from trusting and loving others. Instead of hoping for the best, you'll expect the worst. If the root of bitterness is not removed, an attitude of cynicism will begin to rule your thinking.

Please realize that holding a grudge only holds you back. So stop replaying the offense over and over again in your mind. You'll only truly be free when you make the choice to forgive.

Symptom 5: BLAMING OTHERS

Another major indicator that you are harboring unforgiveness in your heart is a growing urge to blame others. Blame is the language of bitterness. It includes chronically saying or thinking things like:

- It's your fault.
- You did this to me.
- If only you hadn't... (fill in the blank).
- I hate you.

Sadly, the moment we start blaming is the moment we stop growing. The *blame game* was first played by Adam and Eve in the book of Genesis. When God approached Adam and asked him about his decision to eat the forbidden fruit, he responded, "...The woman whom You gave to be with me, she gave me from the tree, and I ate" (Genesis 3:12 NASB). Essentially, Adam said, "It's not my fault! It was my wife's fault! And by the way God, You were the One who gave her to me!" Rather than address the real issue and take responsibility for his actions, Adam chose to play the blame game. As far as he was concerned, it was Eve's fault, God's fault, or both, but it definitely wasn't his fault.

At its core, blame is nothing more than another expression of a prideful heart. It destroys more marriages, churches and businesses than we will probably ever know on this side of heaven. To spend your life blaming the government, the economy, your parents, a former spouse, a past teacher or coach, or even a former pastor only prevents you from making progress and moving forward in your life. John Burroughs said, "You can get discouraged many times, but you are not a failure until you begin to blame somebody else and stop trying".[24]

Unforgiveness has an appetite, and blame is one of its favorite dishes. The more you blame others, the more you feed that stronghold of unforgiveness, and the tighter its grip becomes on your life. The bigger it gets, the harder it becomes to hide. Before you know it, unforgiveness takes over your life and destroys every healthy relationship and opportunity that God brings your way. Friend, this is never what God intended for you.

Symptom 6: SICKNESS

While not all sickness is caused by unforgiveness, unforgiveness can cause sickness. Psalm 38:3 (NLT) says, "...My health is broken because of my sins." There are negative consequences to our decision to withhold forgiveness from someone who's hurt us, and science confirms this as fact. Research shows that unforgiveness causes stress, anxiety, depression, premature aging, arthritis, high blood pressure and some forms of heart disease. As a matter of fact, did you know that unforgiveness is actually classified in medical books as a disease?

It's documented that about 61 percent of cancer patients have forgiveness issues. Steven Stanford, the chief of surgery at the Cancer Treatment Centers of America, reports that "Unforgiveness is known to get and keep people sick." To combat its effects in cancer patients, some doctors and caregivers have started implementing a technique called *forgiveness therapy* as a means to help them beat the disease.[25]

Unforgiveness not only affects the spirit and body, it also affects the mind, eating up your mental bandwidth. You'll constantly find yourself thinking about the person that hurt you as you replay their offense in your mind over and over again. Every time you replay it, the deeper the roots of bitterness grow. What's the remedy to this source of sickness? You guessed it—forgive the person who hurt you.

Karen Swartz, the Director of Mood Disorders at Johns Hopkins Hospital, reports that forgiving someone can actually promote good health. She said that forgiveness promotes, "... lowering the risk of heart attack; improving cholesterol levels and sleep; and reducing pain, blood pressure, and levels of anxiety, depression and stress."[26] The truth is, forgiveness is one of the healthiest gifts that we get to give ourselves.

The longer you refuse to forgive, the more difficult it becomes to forgive. The apostle Paul tells us of the dangers of repeatedly ignoring God's Word and call to forgive. It is like having our conscience "seared as with a hot iron" so that we can't feel the loving correction of God's Holy Spirit any more (see 1 Timothy 4:1-2 KJV).

Are you beginning to see the deadly consequences of unforgiveness? Are you starting to understand how the thought that *Forgiveness Is Optional* is a doorway to a downward spiral you don't want to walk through? Are you ready, with the help of Jesus, to make the choice to forgive?

Practical Steps to Walk in Forgiveness

The deadly thought that *Forgiveness Is Optional* can be devastating unless it's dealt with. God wants you to move forward into the good things He has planned for your life. However, it's hard to experience the blessings of the future while being chained to the pain of your past. Like the apostle Paul, God wants you living your life "forgetting what lies behind and reaching forward to what lies ahead" (Philippians 3:13 NASB). Indeed, Paul's words are some of the best, Holy Spirit-inspired, life advice on the planet.

"But how can I forgive?" you may ask. "They have hurt me so deeply, and I just don't feel like forgiving them." I know it is not easy. I have been hurt deeply by others as well—some who were very close to me. But I learned that forgiveness is not a feeling— it is a *decision*. If you will make the decision to forgive, God will supply the strength you need to carry it out. Let me summarize the steps to forgiveness. This is a prayer you can pray to deal with unforgiveness toward anyone who has offended you:

1) **PRAY FOR STRENGTH:**
   "Lord, please give me the strength, Your strength, to forgive (say person's name). Just as You have extended

tremendous grace towards me, help me to extend grace towards them."

2) **DECIDE TO FORGIVE**:
"As an act of my will and in obedience to Your Word, I choose to forgive (say person's name)."

3) **RELEASE YOUR OFFENDER**:
"You are the Judge, Lord, not me. I release (say person's name) and this entire situation into Your hands."

4) **BLESS YOUR OFFENDER**:
"Lord, although I may not feel like blessing (say person's name) right now, You said to bless them. So by faith, I pray Your blessings upon (say person's name)."

(With God's grace, ask for the good things you would like to see in your life to happen in their life. This principle is found in 1 Peter 3:9-12.)

Are you ready to move forward? You were made for so much more than a life in bondage to unforgiveness. Choosing to walk in forgiveness daily is one of the most liberating choices you will ever make. Realize that forgiveness doesn't release the other person from the responsibility of what they did to you. It releases *you* from what they did to you. If you're serious about tearing down this stronghold in your life, take some time right now to pray and walk through the steps of forgiveness. Ask God to give you the strength to let go of the past. *Choose* to forgive the people you need to forgive. And ask God to forgive you for the people you've hurt.

Then, move forward.

Taking it Captive:

1 – God wants us to treat unforgiveness in our heart like spiritual cancer. He wants to help us deal with it and get free from it. Be still for a moment and pray: "Lord, is there anyone I am offended with? Is there anyone who has hurt me that I am struggling to forgive?" As you sit quietly, jot down the names of anyone who comes to mind.

_____

_____

_____

_____

_____

Carefully reread Jesus' parable of the Unmerciful Servant in Matthew 18:21-35 and His words in Matthew 6:14-15. What is the Holy Spirit speaking to you? How do these scriptures motivate you to release and forgive those who hurt you?

_____

_____

_____

_____

_____

For further study: Ephesians 4:32; Colossians 3:12-13; 1 Peter 3:8-9

2 – A person who is unwilling to forgive is a person who has forgotten what God has forgiven them of. Look back over your life. What are some habits and behaviors for which you're grateful that God has forgiven you? How does remembering these things encourage you to forgive?

_____

_____

_____

_____

_____

3 – Now pray, "Lord, is there anyone *I* have offended? Is there someone *I have hurt* with my words or actions who is struggling to forgive me?" As you sit quietly, jot down the names of anyone who comes to mind. What action(s) is the Holy Spirit prompting you to take?

_____

_____

_____

_____

_____

Take a moment to read Jesus' words in Mark 11:25 and Matthew 18:15-17. What can you learn from these passages about dealing with offense toward those close to you?

_____

_____

_____

_____

_____

4 – To want to pay someone back for the wrong they did is natural. However, God wants us to respond differently. Check out these passages on revenge. What is God revealing to you?

Leviticus 19:18 • Proverbs 20:22; 24:29 • Hebrews 10:30-31 • Romans 12:18-21 • 1 Peter 3:9-12
I believe God is showing me through these passages...

_____

_____

_____

_____

The verses that encourage me most are...

_____

_____

_____

_____

Chapter 10

"IF IT WERE GOD'S WILL, IT WOULD BE EASY"

DEADLY THOUGHT #7: THE STRONGHOLD OF COMFORT

Dear friends, don't be surprised at the fiery trials you are going through, as if something strange were happening to you.
~1 Peter 4:12 (NLT)

Comfort is overrated. It doesn't lead to happiness. It makes us lazy and forgetful. It often leads to self-absorption, boredom, and discontent.[27]

~ Michael Hyatt

The seventh deadly thought we want to examine is a peculiar one. It is the mindset that thinks *If It Were God's Will, It Would Be Easy*. It may be that you are reading this, and your destiny lies dormant—not because God has forsaken or forgotten you, but because Satan has convinced you that if something were God's will for your life, it would be easy. Somehow, he has tricked you into believing that your purpose would be delivered on a cushion of ease and convenience, and that everyone would like you, agree with you, support you, and fight for you. Consequently, you have imagined the door to your destiny opening wide like the gates at the Magic Kingdom—and your walking through it without having to even touch the knob.

In reality, that is not how pursuing your purpose works. When we believe the lie that *If It Were God's Will, It Would Be Easy,* we will quit every time we run into an obstacle or experience some form of resistance. I've even heard many believers spiritualize their decision to retreat when they run up against a wall, saying things like, "It just wasn't God's will," or, "It wasn't meant to be." To this I respond:

"What if it *was* meant to be? What if the opposition is *proof* it is God's will?"

What if your destiny is waiting behind a door that you've walked away from simply because it didn't open the first time you knocked? What if the ministry, career or marriage that God's called you to is waiting for you in the very place He spoke to you about, but you quit too soon because you believed the lie that *If It Were God's Will, It Would Be Easy*?

Jesus Himself told us that "...Here on earth you will have many trials and sorrows..." (John 16:33 NLT). In other words, adversity is actually promised to us. No matter how much we pray, read our Bible, or fast, if we're serious about following Christ and pursuing our purpose, we're going to experience troubles.

For example, when it comes to financial provision, I believe if what we're doing is God's will, it's God's bill. However, that doesn't mean He always pays the bill up front. Sometimes He allows us to be tested with financial leanness to let us see whether or not we'll trust Him to come through with the right amount at the right time, even when no source of provision is in sight.

To be clear, it is totally unbiblical to equate being in God's will with the absence of warfare. In fact, just the opposite is often the case, and few people in Scripture confirm this truth more clearly than the apostle Paul.

Was Paul in God's Will?

In 2 Corinthians 11, Paul gives an overview of some of the adversity he faced on the road to fulfilling his God-given purpose. For starters, his own friends slandered him at times, and others threatened to kill him. He stated that he had been whipped and put into prison so many times he lost count. Five times the Jewish leaders gave him thirty-nine lashes with a whip, and three times he was beaten with rods. Once he was actually dragged out of a city and stoned until they thought he was dead. On top of all this, he experienced going days without food, clothing, and sleep. Paul actually reported being shipwrecked three times. This doesn't mean that the sail blew off the boat or that the engine ran out of gas three times. Shipwrecked means that Paul was stuck in storms so severe that the ship literally fell apart and was lost at sea. He faced the danger of death by drowning three separate times. Yet the entire time Paul was going through all these things, he was in pursuit of the will of God for his life.

Just imagine treading water in the middle of the night, clinging to pieces of broken wood in cold, stormy seas as waves crashed overhead. That's what happened to Paul—not once, not twice, but three times. Interestingly, not once is it recorded in Scripture that Paul had wondered if he was in the will of God. Not once does it say Paul thought to himself, *This must not be God's will for my life, because if it was God's will for me to go to Rome and stand before Caesar, it would be easy*. We also never see Paul in the middle of the sea pounding his fist into the water shouting, "This is ridiculous! Being shipwrecked once is one thing, but three times! I must have heard God wrong. That's it—I quit!"

Although it wasn't easy, we never see Paul allowing difficulties to dictate his destiny. He knew that he was in the will of God despite many life-threatening challenges. Today, if there is even a hint of inconvenience, many believers tend to change their plans. We live in a time where some won't even go to church if the A/C isn't working. The kind of resolve Paul had is quite hard to imagine or understand. I've seen people start to pursue their purpose with infectious passion, only to walk away from their God-given destiny because the process got a little hard.

For the person held captive by the stronghold of comfort, the following scenarios are common:

- Starting a new job with aspirations of turning it into a career, but quitting soon afterward because you don't like your manager.
- Falling in love and getting married with dreams of happiness and romance, but after hitting a rough patch in the relationship, you quickly file for a divorce.
- Going to college to prepare yourself for a prosperous future, but after running into one class or professor that's very challenging, you change your major or quit school altogether.
- Planting a church with an inspiring vision and tons of passion; but after running into a few difficult people who try to subvert the vision by posting unkind words on Facebook, you leave the ministry.

The reason people quit when things get hard is because somewhere along the way people started to believe that *If It Were God's Will, It Would Be Easy*, and this is simply not true.

Perfection Is Not Required

Paul wasn't the only person who had to move past some stormy weather to fulfill his destiny. Peter did too. Before he stepped out of the boat, the only thing He needed to know was whether or not taking the step of faith onto the water was the will of God. So he asked Jesus, "'Lord, if it is You, command me to come to You on the water. And He said, 'Come!...'" (Matthew 14:28-29 NASB).

The moment Peter knew that stepping out of the boat was in his destiny, he swung his feet over the side and stepped out on the water—storm and all. The greatest miracles often happen in the most difficult seasons. There couldn't have possibly been a worse time to try walking on water. Waves were crashing over the ship, the wind was blowing so hard that they couldn't keep the boat pointed in the right direction, and they were too far away from shore to swim to safety. Yet it was in that very moment that Peter stepped out of the boat.

He didn't wait for calm waters, nor did he ask Jesus to first calm the seas and stop the storm. Instead, he stepped out of the boat in the midst of it all, demonstrating that God doesn't need perfect circumstances in order to perform the miraculous in our lives.

He doesn't need the right people to like you or believe in you to get you in position for your purpose. He also doesn't need you to have more money in the bank or have a more impressive resume. All God needs is for you to trust Him and be willing to walk through a storm if necessary to accomplish His will and discover His best for your life. That is what Peter did.

There's something else I love about Peter's walking on the water. The Bible says that after he willingly stepped out of the boat, about halfway across he stopped focusing on Jesus and started focusing on the storm. Suddenly, the waves seemed too high and the wind too strong. When Peter focused on the difficulty rather than his destiny, he started sinking. Frightened, he cried out, "Lord, save me!" (Matthew 14:30) Immediately, Jesus grabbed him and pulled him into the boat. The reason I love this part of the story is that it shows us that not only does Jesus not need perfect circumstances, He also doesn't need perfect people. We may get our focus off of what He's called us to, but He can still lift us up and give us a chance to try it again.

Pain = Preparation for Your Destination

There's purpose in our pain. Pain often purifies our motives and produces the strength we will need to carry the weight of glory to which God has called us. Second Corinthians 4:17 (NKJV) says, "For our light affliction, which is but for a moment, is working for us a far more exceeding and eternal weight of glory." And 1 Peter 5:10 says, "After you have suffered for a little while, the God of all grace, who called you to His eternal glory in Christ, will Himself perfect, confirm, strengthen and establish you" (NASB). In other words, our pain today prepares us for our purpose tomorrow.

The painful seasons are often our perfecting seasons. Satan will try to cause us to believe just the opposite. He'll try to convince us that the difficulty we're facing is proof that we heard God wrong or that the timing just isn't right. He'll attempt to use pain against us to alienate us from God. Satan wants us to believe that God is indifferent toward us and that He doesn't really care—that He is angry with us or even that He has stopped loving us. None of these are true.

The truth is, while God your Father didn't send the pain, He'll use it for your good. He'll use the pain you're going through to reveal that when you feel weak, He'll be your strength. He's teaching you about His love and faithfulness. He's showing you that He can take what the enemy meant for evil and use it for your good. God's not punishing you; He's lovingly preparing you for your purpose.

Oftentimes we think we're strong, until something goes wrong. It's been said that adversity introduces a man to himself, and I believe it's true. God uses adversity to reveal our weaknesses and show us the areas of our lives in which we have yet to truly put our trust in Him beyond what we can see, how we feel, or what others say.

The reality is, pain has become an enemy of sorts, and to a degree I get it. Who likes pain? Most of us spend our lives trying to avoid it. Unfortunately, we cannot give birth to our purpose any more than a mother can give birth to her child without experiencing some pain. Like it or not, pain is built into the process, and to spend our lives trying to avoid it is to avoid life itself.

When my wife was in labor with our daughter, I remember her looking at me after pushing for awhile and saying, "I can't do this anymore. I'm tired, and I don't have anything left. I can't give birth to this baby." Later on after it was all over, I remember her saying to me, "What was I thinking? Of course I was going to give birth! In that pain, I didn't feel like I could make it, but what else was going to happen? Was the baby going to stay in my womb forever? Of course not."

When you're in the midst of pain, it will cause you to believe the enemy's lies are true. He will try to get you to believe the *I Can't Do It* lie, the *I Don't Have What It Takes* lie, and he'll try to convince you that you can't take anymore. But pain can also be very deceptive.

Realize it's often when you're at the threshold of giving birth to something that you experience the most pain and are tempted to quit. But there's something beautiful on the other side of that pain. There's life, purpose, and destiny like you've never known before if you'll just keep pushing. In his book *Leadership Pain*, Dr. Sam Chand said it this way: "...Pain isn't the enemy. The unwillingness to face pain is a far greater danger."[28] I agree.

Until your frustration with your own progress becomes greater than your fear of pain, you'll never step into your purpose. Pain has been and always will be a part of the process. If you don't understand this, you'll always view pain as proof that you should quit, back up, and forget about the things God has placed in your heart. As a result, you'll go through life carrying great potential, but never stepping into it. You'll instinctively know that something's close, but you'll never see it materialize. The *If It Were God's Will, It Would Be Easy* lie will dominate and defeat you. This is not what God intends for your life.

The Three C's of a Counterfeit Purpose

In an attempt to keep us from fulfilling our purpose, the enemy will subtly introduce the *Three C's of a Counterfeit Purpose*: comfort, cash, and convenience. He uses these as decoys to numb our senses to the true, and sometimes challenging, will of God. They're a sort of false litmus test. In other words, if we sense that what God is asking us to do is not *comfortable*, is not producing abundant *cash*, or doesn't seem *convenient*, we might wrongly assume that it's not God's will. Sadly, if we don't have at least two of these three elements, we often dismiss the true will of God as being the counterfeit.

At first glance, we might actually interpret comfort, cash, and convenience as being from God if we're not careful. While none of these is inherently evil, if any of them are allowed to keep us from our purpose, they can be destructive. Therefore, we must learn how to recognize them and understand how the enemy uses them so they don't pose a threat to our potential.

Let's take a look at each of these.

1. COMFORT

Nowhere in the Bible does Jesus promise that life will always be easy or pain-free. On the contrary, He promised that we'd face troubles and adversity (see John 16:33). The truth of the matter is, God isn't interested in our comfort. He's interested in our obedience. Many of us are being held captive by the enemy of comfort. As a result, we filter the opportunities that come our way through how comfortable we think they will make us. We only step into opportunities that we feel we're competent to fulfill without a possibility of failure. The problem with this mindset is that it doesn't allow us to grow. We can't learn anything new or stretch to our full potential if there is no challenge. If we only do what we've always done, we'll only get what we've always got.

For the disciples, leaving their families, friends, and jobs to follow a man they had just met wasn't comfortable. Likewise, it wasn't comfortable for Noah to build a boat and prepare for the coming deluge of rain, neither of which he had ever seen. And for Jesus, the cross and the cruelty that came before it weren't comfortable, yet He had to endure it in order to fulfill His destiny. I once heard Bishop Dale C. Bronner, the senior pastor of Word of Faith Family Worship Cathedral say, "Sometimes God delivers you from the fiery furnace; other times He makes you fireproof—you must endure it! God is more concerned with your development than He is with your comfort."[29]

While we are not promised comfort on the road to fulfilling our destiny, we are promised God's continual abiding presence and deliverance—either *from* life's troubles or *through* them. King David said it this way, "Many are the afflictions of the righteous, but the Lord delivers him out of them all" (Psalm 34:19 NKJV).

Is your refusal to step outside of your comfort zone keeping you from taking hold "of that for which Christ Jesus took hold of" you? (Philippians 3:12 NIV) Don't let lack of comfort keep you from fulfilling your calling. I dare you to step outside of your comfort zone and follow Jesus.

2. CASH

Although money is great, cash is not king. Only Jesus can fulfill the role of King in our lives. I have watched the issue of money hold many people back from the will of God. They tragically try to discern God's will based on how much money they will make. For instance, I've seen men and women in ministry decide whether they were going to pastor a church or not based on the salary and benefit package being offered. I've also seen people who were thriving in the will of God for their life abandon their divine calling on account of money.

The Bible has much to say about money. Yet God never said, "You'll know which door to walk through by the size of the salary being offered." Scripture does warn us that, "...The love of money is a root of all kinds of evil. Some people, eager for money, have wandered from the faith and pierced themselves with many griefs" (1 Timothy 6:10 NIV). And Jesus said, "No one can serve two masters. Either you will hate the one and love the other, or you will be devoted to the one and despise the other. You cannot serve both God and money" (Luke 16:13 NIV). The disciples left everything to follow Jesus. Not for the promise of a great salary package and insurance benefits. It was because they heard Jesus' divine call saying, "Come!"

Personally, I still believe in the call of God. On two separate occasions, I've been afforded the divine opportunity to pastor the Lord's church. In both cases, I intentionally refused to inquire beforehand about how much I would be getting paid. I didn't want that distraction. I simply wanted to know one thing: "Lord, is this Your will for my family and me? If it is, then You already have the money issue worked out."

I can't help but wonder how many miracle moments people have missed because they turned down God-opportunities due to what they perceived to be a lack of money. Remember, if it's God's will, it's God's bill. While He doesn't always pay the bill up front, He'll always provide on time. His Word says:

> "...God will generously provide all you need. Then you will always have everything you need and plenty left over to share with others."
>
> **—2 Corinthians 9:8 NLT**

> "...God will meet all your needs according to the riches of his glory in Christ Jesus."
>
> **—Philippians 4:19 NIV**

> "Even strong young lions sometimes go hungry, but those who trust in the Lord will lack no good thing."
>
> **—Psalm 34:10 NLT**

Be careful not to confuse God's promise of provision with making money. Rest assured, God will meet your needs. His provision may not always come in the package you recognize or at the time you desire. Nevertheless, it will come because He is faithful. Refuse to make money the main thing. Using cash to discern God's will for your life can eventually result in forfeiting His will for your life.

3. CONVENIENCE

Along with comfort and cash, *convenience* is also an element the enemy uses to establish a counterfeit calling. We live in a world where people want everything their way and in their timing. Like the song says, "I want it all, I want it all, and I want it now!" Think about it. We conveniently connect with people on social media. We conveniently shop online. We conveniently go through the fast-food drive-thru so we don't have to get out of our car to get our coffee or burger. If something is inconvenient, we're more apt to say no to it and wait until something more convenient comes along. There is nothing inherently wrong with things being convenient. However, when it comes to discerning and fulfilling God's will for your life, it will require you to be inconvenienced at times.

When I started in ministry, I pastored a church that was about an hour away from our house. My family and I commuted at least twice a week to the church—once on Wednesday and once on Sunday. Some weeks we made a third trip for meetings or appointments. During that time I also worked fifty to sixty hours a week at another job to pay our bills. The church consisted of only fourteen people, and they weren't even able to pay for my gas to and from church.

A typical workday at my job started at 5 am and ended at 4:30 pm. I'd then run home, take a quick shower, eat dinner on the way to the town where our church was located, and make it just in time for our 7 pm Wednesday night Bible study. Our kids would have to do their homework in the car, and Tina, who really didn't like driving or dealing with expressway traffic, would do most of the driving so that I could study my notes for the message I was about to deliver. Once the Bible study was done, we'd leave the church and usually get home around 10 pm and in bed by 11 pm. I was then up early the next morning so I could be to work by 5 am. Can you say *inconvenient*? Nevertheless, my wife and I never interpreted the lack of cash, comfort, or convenience as a sign that what we were doing wasn't God's will for our lives.

Make no mistake. Fulfilling the call of God on your life will require you to be inconvenienced. When God told Israel to cross into the Promised Land, the Bible says they had to cross when the Jordan River was at flood stage—a very inconvenient time. After Peter had been fishing all night, he was exhausted and ready to wash his nets, go home, and go to sleep. But at that moment, Jesus asked him if He could use his boat. It was an extremely inconvenient time for Peter, but he obeyed Jesus, and it changed his life.

I'm sure it wasn't convenient for David the shepherd boy to kill the bear, the lion, or the giant Goliath. Nor was it convenient for a virgin named Mary to conceive and carry a child, having to explain to her family and friends, "It's okay. I'm still a virgin. This is actually God's Son I'm carrying."

How about Jesus? He left the paradise of Heaven, came to fallen earth, and took all our sins upon Himself. He was beaten beyond recognition, spit upon and crowned with thorns, and He died a cruel death on the cross before rising again. Nothing seems very convenient in His story.

My point is, don't let convenience keep you from walking in the will of God and experiencing His promises. Scripture says, "If you wait for perfect conditions, you will never get anything done" (Ecclesiastes 11:4 TLB). If you have created a list of personal conveniences you require God to meet before you obey His will for your life, then you might miss His best for you. Yes, initially it may be very inconvenient to carry out His plan, but the rewards far outweigh the struggle. Trust me.

Now that we've examined the *Three C's of a Counterfeit Purpose*, let's take a look at the *Three C's of a Kingdom Calling*.

The Three C's of a Kingdom Calling

1. THE CALLING

Second Timothy 1:9 (NIV) is one of many verses revealing our divine calling. It says, "He has saved us and *called* us to a holy life—not because of anything we have done but because of his own purpose and grace. This grace was given us in Christ Jesus before the beginning of time."

For Paul the call was enough. One word from Jesus on a Damascus Road was enough for him to walk away from everything with no guarantees of anything. Oftentimes we, too, hear God's call, but we put off answering that call by saying, "I'm waiting for a confirmation." Then when we get one, we ask for another... and then another.

The truth is we're not waiting for a confirmation. We're waiting for someone to promise us that it will be easy. We want the guarantees of comfort, cash, and convenience before we answer that call. Thankfully, God can bring us to the place where, like Paul, we count everything of this world as rubbish in comparison to knowing and gaining Christ! (See Philippians 3:8.) God will supply all you need to answer His call on your life.

2. The Cost

Looking back over the course of my life, I've discovered that answering God's call is the easy part; it's walking it out that's costly. Personally, I've been betrayed, lied about, misunderstood, misrepresented, and even slandered. Sometimes it comes from the very people you love and lead, while other times it emerges from your peers in the form of jealousy, insecurity, and an unhealthy kind of religious competition. Either way, if you're committed to answering God's call and making a difference in the world, you're going to experience disappointment and criticism. At times you'll be tempted to quit, stop trusting people, or build emotional walls to keep people out and play it safe. Some days it feels like the more you try to help people and fulfill the will of God for your life, church, or organization, the less people appreciate it. I've been there.

Because of all the above, you'll be tempted more than once in your life to quit on your calling. You'll contemplate throwing in the towel and walking away because it seems too hard, and you wonder if all the frustration and pain are worth it. Let me share something with you that's a game changer. It's an axiom I live by, and it's completely transformed the way I perceive the dark seasons and disappointments of life. Here it is: nothing happens *to* you, it happens *for* you!

James 1:2-3 (NIV), "Consider it pure joy, my brothers and sisters, whenever you face trials of many kinds, because you know that the testing of your faith produces perseverance." For your good, God uses absolutely everything the enemy intended for evil. He harnesses it to produce something good in you, and He doesn't waste anything you've been through. He redeems every ounce of adversity to help you fulfill your God-given purpose and calling. Yes, there's a cost, but walking in your purpose is worth the price because, in the end, the price you paid produced the results that you wanted. You learn that it's His strength and not yours that will see you through. You learn that God really is for you and that He's moving all of the pieces into place in order to give you the abundant life He wants you to have.

3. THE COMMITMENT

Dedication, loyalty, devotion, steadfastness, allegiance, and faithfulness—all words that describe and define the word *commitment*. In Luke 9:62 (NIV), Jesus said "No one who puts a hand to the plow and looks back is fit for service in the kingdom of God." This is a picture of commitment—a forward focus on Christ and His calling. Without commitment, we will retreat at the first sign of adversity. Without commitment, we'll interpret difficulty as God's disapproval. And then we'll spiritualize our desertion by labeling difficulty as a closed door. However, running into difficulty doesn't necessarily mean you've reached a door that God has closed. It may just be that you've bought the lie that *open* door equals *easy* door.

Interestingly, when Paul described the open door before him, the word easy was nowhere to be found. He said, "...A great door for effective work has opened to me, and there are many who oppose me" (1 Corinthians 16:9 NIV). Fact: When doors open, opposition arises. It is commitment that keeps us in the game. Some of us are postponing our purpose because we won't commit ourselves to the process.

If anyone was committed, it was the apostle Paul. Scripture says he went through a terrible storm, the ship was wrecked, and it almost cost him his life. Yet he did it again. He went through a second storm, the ship was wrecked, and it almost cost him his life. And he did it again. He went through a third storm, the ship was wrecked, and it almost cost him his life. Yet he did it again. On his fourth attempt, the ship stayed intact, and he made it to his destination.

God never promised that life would be storm-free, and He never said that you wouldn't experience pain on the road to pursuing your purpose. However, He did promise in His Word that it would all be worth it. He said, "And we know that God causes all things to work together for good to those who love God, to those who are called according to His purpose" (Romans 8:28 NASB). God's purpose for your life is far too important to allow comfort, cash, and convenience to keep you from your calling.

Refuse to let the stronghold of comfort take you prisoner. Tear it down by taking the *If It Were God's Will, It Would Be Easy* thought captive to the obedience of Christ! No, your life will not always be easy, and you will not always be comfortable. Nevertheless...

> "God blesses those who patiently endure testing and temptation. Afterward they will receive the crown of life that God has promised to those who love him."
>
> **—James 1:12 (NLT)**

What's more...

> "...No eye has seen, no ear has heard, and no mind has imagined what God has prepared for those who love him."
>
> **—1 Corinthians 2:9 (NLT)**

TAKING IT CAPTIVE:

1 – Be honest. Have you ever thought, *If it were God's will, it would be easy*? Are you believing this right now? If so, what have you heard or read in the past that would cause you to believe *ease equals the will of God*? How has this chapter helped you see things more accurately?

_____

_____

_____

_____

_____

2 – Of the *Three C's of a Counterfeit Purpose*, which one tends to be the most challenging: comfort, cash, or convenience? Why would you say this is the case? What adjustments in your perception do you need the Holy Spirit to help you make?

_____

_____

_____

_____

_____

3 – To the best of your understanding, describe what you feel in your heart that God has called you to do in your current season of life. Are you still pursuing this purpose? If not, why have you walked away from it? What action(s) is the Holy Spirit prompting you to take?

_____

_____

_____

_____

_____

4 – What you're focusing on powerfully affects the level of strength and faith you experience as you daily walk out your calling. Carefully read Hebrews 3:1-2 and 12:2-3; Matthew 11:28-30. What is the Holy Spirit showing you in these passages?

_____

_____

_____

_____

5 – To help us verify God's will for our lives—in both big and small decisions—He has given us two major indicators to confirm He is directing us: *peace* and *faith*. Take a few moments and meditate on Colossians 3:15 and Romans 14:23 below. Then write what God is showing you about how His peace and faith direct our decisions.

> "And let the peace (soul harmony which comes) from Christ rule (act as umpire continually) in your hearts [deciding and settling with finality all questions that arise in your minds, in that peaceful state] to which as [members of Christ's] one body you were also called [to live]..."
>
> **—Colossians 3:15 AMPC**

"But the man who has doubts (misgivings, an uneasy conscience) about eating, and then eats... stands condemned [before God], because he is not true to his convictions and he does not act from faith. For whatever does not originate and proceed from faith is sin [whatever is done without a conviction of its approval by God is sinful]."

—Romans 14:23 AMPC

I believe God is showing me through these passages...

_____

_____

_____

_____

_____

Chapter 11

WINNING THE WAR
FOR YOUR MIND

*"...and we take captive every thought
to make it obedient to Christ."
~ 2 Corinthians 10:5 NIV*

"Men are not prisoners of fate, but only prisoners
of their own minds"[30]

~Franklin D. Roosevelt

Old deadly thought patterns aren't going down without a fight. Satan, the enemy of your soul, doesn't want you to begin thinking God's higher thoughts about your marriage, career, ministry, money, or anything else. He and his demonic cronies will stop at nothing to try and prevent you from discovering your God-ordained purpose and potential. You are on notice: the battlefield is your mind—the place where more purpose has perished and dreams have died than any other place in the history of mankind. In a spiritual sense, it's a battlefield that has claimed more lives than Gettysburg or the beaches of Normandy combined.

In her best-selling book *The Battlefield of the Mind*, teacher and author Joyce Meyer writes:

"We are in a war...not with other human beings but with the devil and his demons...He begins by bombarding our mind with a cleverly devised pattern of little nagging thoughts, suspicions, doubts, fears, wonderings, reasonings, and theories. He moves slowly and cautiously (after all, well-laid plans take time). Remember, he has a strategy for his warfare. He has studied us for a long time. He knows what we like and what we don't like. He knows our insecurities, our weaknesses, and our fears. He knows what bothers us most. He is willing to invest any amount of time it takes to defeat us...**Satan knows well that if he can control our thoughts, he can control our actions** [emphasis mine]."[31]

Indeed, Satan knows all too well that our thoughts are directly tied to our actions, so the moment we get ready to take a step of faith in the right direction, he launches a toxic attack against our mind. He introduces deceptive thoughts designed to pull us in the opposite direction of our purpose. The apostle Paul describes this inner battle in Romans 7, noting that there is a power "...at war with my mind." Why Satan fights so fiercely will be revealed in the pages that follow. We will pull the curtain back and see how he operates as the *thief* described by Jesus in John 10:10, how new thoughts won't fit into an old mind, and how renewing our minds is both life-changing and required to win the war. First, let's begin by reviewing what it means to be enslaved by low thinking.

Enslaved By Low Thinking

In his book *Instinct*, pastor and best-selling author Bishop T.D. Jakes gives us a sobering example of the power of thinking *higher thoughts* and the warfare that the enemy will launch against you in order to keep you enslaved to low thinking about yourself and about your purpose.

"In the dark history of the formation of our country, the enslaved were forbidden to learn how to read. The slave owners of that time understood all too well: the key to freedom was in the mind of the enslaved. Once the person in bondage thought like a free being, they would be nearly impossible to control. If you liberate someone's thinking, it is only a matter of time before chains cannot hold their liberated mentality."[32]

Every low thought is a link in the chain holding you captive to a lesser version of yourself. No matter what part of your life Satan's coming after right now, he knows that the key to his success is always found in attacking the way you *think* about yourself and God in that specific area of your life. In order to prevent you from thinking higher thoughts, he'll point out everything you *don't* have in order to keep you from realizing what you *do* have. He'll remind you of all the people that *don't* believe in you in order to keep you from seeing and finding the ones who *do* believe in you. He has mastered the art of overwhelming you with a flood of thoughts that highlight all of your weaknesses until you've completely forgotten all of your God-given strengths. His aim is to keep you enslaved to your *low places* by wrapping his chains of *low thinking* around your mind. He knows all too well that the moment your thinking is liberated, those shackles will no longer be able to keep you enslaved to your past failures, defeats, shortcomings, and deceptions.

In a 2015 Ted Talk entitled "Draw Your Future," Patti Dobrowolski offered a vivid example of the power of a stronghold and just how tightly the chains of low-thinking can wrap themselves around our minds. She reported that "...the odds of you actually changing your life is 9 to 1; even when faced with a life-threatening illness."[33] Wow! How can our inability to make life-saving changes, even in the face of certain death, be explained any other way than a spiritual stronghold? The reason the odds are so highly stacked against us is that we keep trying to change our lives without first changing our minds.

The good news is that the odds presented in the study didn't take into account the life-transforming power of Jesus Christ and the billions of lives that have been transformed by allowing Him to "renew" their minds. The odds also failed to include the fact that "God is for you," according to Romans 8:31, and that "No weapon formed against you shall prosper," as declared by the Lord Himself in Isaiah 54:17 (NKJV). So no matter how long you've been fighting this battle for your mind, don't quit. God is fighting for you, and as long as you don't quit fighting, you will win!

You Are Intimidating

Spiritual warfare is very real. We should not fear it, but we must be aware that we're in it. Ephesians 6:12 (NASB) reveals, "Our struggle is not against flesh and blood, but against the rulers, against the powers, against the world forces of this darkness, against the spiritual forces of wickedness in heavenly places." One important thing you need to know is this: If Satan *can* use something against you, then you must always assume that he *will*. He'll use your past and your present, your failures and your mistakes, your insecurities and your inferiorities. He doesn't fight fair, and just because you've been forgiven of something doesn't mean that Satan has forgotten about it. Any chance he gets, he will dredge up past failures and use them all against you. If any of these modes of attack sound familiar, then allow me to encourage you with one truth the enemy has worked very hard to keep you from discovering:

"The fact that Satan has fought so hard against you only validates the great plan God has for you!"

Go ahead, read that last statement again. Now I want you to make it personal and say it out loud: "The fact that Satan has fought so hard against *me* only validates the great plan God has for *me*!" By taking ownership of this truth, you have officially started to fight back against the enemy. You are learning a very important part of "...taking every thought captive to the obedience of Christ" (2 Corinthians 10:5 NASB).

In most cases, I believe Satan recognizes our potential long before we do. He makes it his mission to keep us from realizing the vision and purpose for which we were created. He attempts to keep it buried beneath layers of negative thinking. He knows that if we ever start to cultivate the kind of *higher thoughts* that match our God-ordained purpose, we will become dangerous to the powers of darkness. Now you may ask, "Why in the world would the enemy spend so much time and effort trying to attack and intimidate me?" The answer is simple. You intimidate him.

Let me say that if the devil isn't bothering you, then it's probably because you're not bothering the devil. Although I don't think for a moment that all of our problems can or should be blamed on Satan and that far too often he gets the blame for our own bad decisions, I do believe he is the one behind many of the mental attacks we experience. The enemy knows all too well the power of right thinking and the deadly side effects of wrong thinking. That is why he bombards us with the latter. Therefore, we must understand his tactics so that we can learn how to identify a true attack on our thought life and know how to stand against it.

The Thief

In the 2010 movie *Inception*, Leonardo DiCaprio plays the role of Dom Cobb, a uniquely skilled and high-priced thief for hire who has the ability to tap into a person's dreamworld and steal valuable thoughts and information from his victims. His greatest challenge arises when he's hired by a corporate competitor not merely to steal a thought, but rather to *introduce* a thought (hence the title, *Inception*) into the mind of a billionaire's son with the goal of convincing him to break up his father's corporate dynasty.

In the film, the only way this tactic of planting a destructive thought will work is if it's planted deep enough for the victim to take ownership of the thought. This is the thief's greatest challenge—to find a way to convince his victim that the destructive thought being planted is actually his own original idea. If the potential victim realizes the deceptive idea was planted there by an enemy, it would be rejected, and the attack would be thwarted.

Did you catch that interesting mode of operation? Let me say it again: *the challenge for the thief is to find a way to convince his victim that the destructive thought being planted is actually his own original idea, when in fact it isn't. It is the work of an enemy.*

This is exactly how Satan, the *thief*, attacks God's people. According to John 10:10 (NASB), "The thief comes only to steal and kill and destroy...," and he knows all too well that the road to destruction begins with a single thought. He knows that our lives can't be transformed without the "renewing of our minds." Therefore, he stealthily steps onto the battlefield of our mind armed with deadly thoughts of defeat, desperation, and discouragement, disguising all of these thoughts as our own original ideas.

How does Satan move into our mind, whisper destructive thoughts, and convince us those thoughts are our own ideas? The answer is, Satan is not only a thief, but he's also a professional hijacker. He hijacks the sound of your voice and my voice and effectively convinces us that what we're hearing is our own thoughts. Consequently, we take ownership without a second thought. He carefully reaches into his bag of lies and proceeds to fire his thoughts of failure, inadequacy, and condemnation at the most wounded and vulnerable places in our minds. The longer you and I choose to entertain these thoughts, the more we'll begin to believe them, and it's only a matter of time before a stronghold is established. Suddenly, where faith once reigned, fear begins to rule. This is why recognizing and taking wrong thoughts captive is so vital.

With eye-opening accuracy and practical wisdom, Pastor Ron Carpenter addressed the importance of taking every thought captive when he said:

> "It's a proven, scientific fact that when any thought enters your mind, you have approximately 30 seconds to deal with it and make a decision

before your feelings set in. Your mind is given the job of deciding the battle between you and your thoughts. It's up to your mind to control your ideas and imagination and make a decision as to where they'll go next. Here's the danger: After your 30 seconds are up, your emotions kick in and develop a relationship with the thought. You become emotionally invested, and that's when it starts getting complicated...Your thoughts can put you in the worst mood or the best mood; can make yourself the happiest person no matter the condition of your surroundings or hell to live with. Your feelings aren't coming from your surroundings; they're coming directly from your thoughts."[34]

It All Starts with a Thought

Have you ever stopped to consider how many things in life fall apart because of the way we think? Relationships, businesses, ministries, you name it. When it happens, most people respond by diagnosing the outward actions surrounding the situation. However, most of our difficult circumstances didn't start with our actions—they started with our thoughts.

Like accidentally downloading a virus onto the hard drive of your computer, once you've downloaded the wrong thought into the mainframe of your mind, that thought can begin to infect everything it touches. Left unchecked, that free radical of negativity gives birth to a series of low thoughts of defeat, which eventually turn into the corresponding low actions. Unless it is dealt with, a defeated life is sure to follow—a life in which nothing seems to be working out for you. No matter what you do, you just can't seem to regain control of your thinking or pull your life back together. All because you chose to take ownership of a single destructive thought.

Let me explain what I mean by offering these examples:

- Satan doesn't destroy a marriage by introducing a full-blown affair. He simply introduces a destructive thought that says, *I'd be happier with someone else*, or, *I bet he/she would appreciate me more than my spouse.* It's only *after* a person decides to own this kind of thought as their own original idea that they start to pursue an affair and ultimately end up in a divorce.
- Satan usually doesn't destroy a church by sending a band of rebellious people into it to tear it apart. He simply introduces a low thought into the pastor's mind like, *I have arrived!* Once he takes ownership of that thought, Satan hardly has to lift another finger. The pastor becomes prideful and stops learning how to better lead and pastor his church. Or he introduces a thought in the mind of the congregation like, *Why do we need to reach broken people or people that have different struggles than I do – that makes me feel uncomfortable.* It's just a matter of time before these low thoughts turn into low actions, and the ministry becomes nothing more than a religious social club rather than a spiritual hospital where broken people are made well again.

This one might hurt a little, but it's important.

- Satan doesn't necessarily have to inflict sickness or disease upon you to destroy your health. All he has to do is get you to download the destructive thought that says, *Eating right and exercising don't really matter. We all have to go some time, and when it's my time, it's just my time.* If you choose to own that low thought and neglect your physical health (aka the temple of the Holy Spirit), then it won't be long before the low actions of bad eating and little to no exercise take hold, and the enemy accomplishes his mission. Overwhelmed with regret, you'll find yourself utilizing all your energy rebuking a sickness that you yourself invited into your life. And it all started with one destructive thought.

We could go on and on, but I think you get the picture. Destructive thoughts are deadly, and they are fired at each of us every single day. Like torpedoes under the water, they often aren't detected until they burst upon us. The question is, once they arrive, will you take the thought captive to the obedience of Christ? Or will you take the bait and own the deadly thought as your own? It's only when you take ownership of these thoughts that the enemy has succeeded in making a direct hit, and your dreams begin to sink in the ocean of "what could have been."

New Thoughts Won't Fit Into an Old Mind

So we are in a spiritual war against Satan and his demonic hordes. As sons and daughters of God, the enemy is highly intimidated by the dynamic, divine potential residing within you. Therefore, he will stop at nothing to find and feed you the perfect low thought he knows you will accept as your own. His goal is to initiate the systematic dismantling of your God-given destiny. The way to win this war for your mind is to learn to recognize and take captive the enemy's lies parading as truth. The apostle Paul explains:

> "...Though we live in the world, we do not wage war as the world does. The weapons we fight with are not the weapons of the world. On the contrary, they have divine power to demolish strongholds. We demolish arguments and every pretension that sets itself up against the knowledge of God, and we take captive every thought to make it obedient to Christ."

> **—2 Corinthians 10:3-5 (NIV)**

To recognize Satan's lies—his arguments, theories, and thoughts that enter our minds and attempt to usurp the Word of God—we must fill our minds with truth. However, in order for our minds to effectively absorb the truth, we need God to change them. That is, we can't put new thoughts into an old mind. Let me explain.

Jesus's ministry was revolutionary. No one in the world had ever seen someone do what Jesus did. He forgave sins, healed the sick, and raised the dead. He went from a following of twelve disciples to leading thousands of people from all walks of life. The crowds that came to hear the Master preach were massive, and everybody loved what He was doing to change lives! Well, maybe not everybody.

There was a group of men who are identified as Pharisees. They were considered the religious leaders of the day, and they weren't too crazy about Jesus. It wasn't so much *what* Jesus was doing—it was *how* He was doing it. As experts in religious law, they were all about the "do's" and "dont's." They definitely weren't the guys you'd want leading your hospitality ministry at church.

The Pharisees would be equivalent to what I call the modern day "church-cops." You know...the people who seem to make it their life mission to keep track of your church attendance and judge whether or not you meet their criteria of the proper dress code. Yet the Pharisees were far worse.

If you stepped out of line by working on the Sabbath, or you hung out with "unholy" sinners or forgot to exercise the spiritual discipline of fasting, the Pharisees would be the first to speak up and straighten you out. Well, Jesus had a habit of doing all of the above and more. He didn't just heal people. He seemed to go out of His way to heal them on the Sabbath. Likewise, He didn't just choose not to fast. He would openly eat with sinners. And every time a group of Pharisees challenged Jesus, He responded by addressing the real issue—the problem with their thinking.

When the Pharisees questioned why Jesus ate and drank with sinners, Jesus—aka the TRUTH—answered, "It is not those who are healthy who need a physician, but those who are sick" (Matthew 9:12 NASB). When the Pharisees questioned why Jesus' disciples didn't fast the way they and John's disciples did, Jesus— aka the TRUTH—answered, "Can you make the friends of the bridegroom fast while the bridegroom is with them?" (Luke 5:34

NKJV) In other words, what Jesus was saying was, "Hey guys, your thinking about Me and about ministry is backwards."

The reason the Pharisees couldn't accept what Jesus was doing and teaching was that they were thinking with an old mind. They couldn't fit His new thoughts into their old mindset. Jesus explained their problem by saying,

> "No one puts new wine into old wineskins; otherwise the wine will burst the skins, and the wine is lost and the skins as well; but one puts new wine into fresh wineskins."

> **—Mark 2:22 (NASB)**

To truly understand the parallel Jesus was making, let me give you the lowdown on wineskins.

Wineskins were actually leather pouches that held wine. New wine was the juice from freshly crushed grapes. Once new wine was poured into a new wineskin, the fermentation process would cause the skin to stretch and expand. Eventually, as the fermenting concluded, the leather skin would grow dry and hard. You couldn't use a wineskin more than once because after the first use it would have been stretched to the max due to the wine's fermenting. It could stretch no more.

Putting new wine into an old wineskin would cause the hardened, inflexible skin to burst as the new wine started fermenting. Thus, the new wine would leak out, and both the wineskin and the wine would be lost.

Are you seeing the connection? Jesus was indirectly calling the Pharisees old wineskins. They had been mentally stretched to the max by the "old wine" of the law of Moses, unable to receive the new covenant of grace that Jesus was ushering in. Their fear of change left them rigid and inflexible. They were too committed to their traditions and what they had already learned and were unwilling to change their old way of life and ministry in order to be able to receive the "new wine" Jesus offered. They simply couldn't think new thoughts and accept that this man named Jesus was indeed the Messiah they had been waiting and praying for.

Just as old wineskins can't hold new wine, an old, unrenewed mind can't contain new thoughts. No matter how hard we pray, unless we're willing to let God change our minds, we'll never be capable of receiving and thinking higher thoughts.

To be clear, by using the word *old*, I'm not necessarily talking about age. I'm talking about a stubborn *I'll do it the way I've always done it* attitude—one that says, "I don't like change. Keep me comfortable." Being an old wineskin is holding onto the kind of thinking that limits you from receiving the fresh vision and revelation that God wants to pour into your life. It's a mindset that thinks the only way to do things is the way we have always done them.

Ultimately, we are left with a choice: We can either be an old wineskin like the Pharisees—rigid, inflexible, and hardened by our traditions and old ways of thinking. Or we can be like a new wineskin—pliable, flexible, humble, and open to the truth and new things God wants to do in our lives.

Transform Your Mind

The good news is that it's possible to change the way you think. The Bible says that the key to renewing your mind and lining up your thoughts with God's will is only through transformation. Through Paul, God says,

> "...Do not be conformed to this world, but be transformed by the renewing of your mind, so that you may prove what the will of God is, that which is good and acceptable and perfect."

—Romans 12:2 (NASB)

According to this scripture, our ability to discern the perfect will of God, which is good and acceptable, hinges on whether or not we are actively renewing our minds. The moment we stop renewing our minds is the moment rigidity and inflexibility begin to set in. Old, engrained thought patterns will dominate us by default. We cannot afford to be closed to the new, fresh things God is wanting to do in and through us and the Church. We must be transformed by the renewing of our minds every single day.

In his book *The Necessity of an Enemy*, Pastor Ron Carpenter, Jr. examines the power and possibilities of renewing the mind when he writes:

> "I was fascinated to learn from a neurologist one day that the grooves in our brains are thinking patterns. In other words, how you think actually affects the structure of your brain! This neurologist also told me that it's possible for people to rewrite the grooves in their brains if they will accept new patterns of thinking. Your brain, literally and physically, will change in shape and contour if you can release old information and fill your mind with the knowledge of God. Amazing! Good thinking doesn't just change the perception of things; it actually changes the physical mechanism of the brain. Now I see that there's more to this "renewing of your mind" (Romans 12:2) than I realized."[35]

In the church world we often define renewing the mind strictly by reading our Bibles, and while I certainly agree that this plays a huge role in our ability to think higher thoughts, I believe there is more to it. Think about the verse above (Romans 12:2) that Paul wrote to the Roman church. At that time, they didn't have the Bible as we know it today. What Paul was trying to help them do was break out of their spiritual ruts. He was challenging them to change the way they thought about worship, church life, ministry, and living their lives for God. Paul was a trusted mentor, a friend, a pastor, and an apostle writing under the inspiration of the Holy Spirit. He was challenging the people to change those old ways of thinking that were getting in the way of the new things God was trying to accomplish in their lives.

Make no mistake. Renewing our minds includes reading our Bibles, but it also involves seeking out solid, godly friends and mentors who love us enough to challenge our antiquated thinking. It includes reading inspiring books from faithful sources, listening to podcasts, and watching YouTube videos that will challenge our ability to become better people, leaders, servants, and spouses. When the Word of God, a friend, or any of these sources of renewal make us uncomfortable, it is often because they are confronting a weakness in our thinking that needs to change. Addressing the issue will feel unnatural and uneasy at first, but no more unnatural or uneasy than the cross felt to our King. Yes, it will hurt a bit to change our thinking, but it won't hurt as much as the nails piercing the hands and feet of Jesus in order to bring about the greatest change in the history of the world.

You Have Permission from God

There's one more thing you need to know when it comes to renewing your mind and thinking higher thoughts, and that is to realize that not everyone will be in agreement with you. In fact, sometimes those closest to you will not understand why you are thinking the way you are thinking, and that's okay.

I remember being in the middle of a season of intense frustration. I was trying to share my vision with some leaders, but they just couldn't seem to grasp what I was wanting to do and to rally around it. Deeply discouraged, I began to think, *Maybe my peers are right and it's ridiculous to think that anything could change for the better. Maybe I'm expecting too much, and I just need to get my head out of the clouds.*

Just as I was about to wave the white flag of surrender over my idea, I heard God speak in a still small voice and say, *Travis, I'm giving you a strong warning not to think like everyone else does. I've created you to think differently.* Those words ignited a fire in my bones. They are the reason that this book is in your hands.

As soon as I heard God speak them, I went home and began scouring the Scriptures for any verse that would confirm, or at least correlate, with the truth God had just dropped into my heart. For about ten minutes I searched frantically. Then, low and behold, I found it. God had uttered these same powerful words to someone else. His name was Isaiah, and as far as I can tell, the first time God spoke it was about 3,000 years ago. Isaiah wrote:

> "The Lord has given me a strong warning not to think like everyone else does..."

—Isaiah 8:11 (NLT)

There it was in black and white. I'm sure God has probably said it countless times to other men and women throughout the centuries who've struggled with discouraging and self-defeating thoughts, but for me in that moment, His words were life-transforming!

There are two powerful principles God showed me in this verse. First, He gave Isaiah a strong warning not to fall into the trap of thinking like everybody else. The second principle is not written, but implied, and it is that God gave Isaiah *permission to think differently*. Now, these instructions were not just for Isaiah, and they were not just for me. The fact that they are in the Word of God means that they are for everyone who calls on the name of Jesus.

Like Isaiah, you and I can never become who God created us to be by thinking like everyone else thinks. God strongly warned us not to. Yet with the warning comes permission to start thinking higher thoughts like Him, our Father in Heaven.

Yes, you may be called radical at first for trying to think higher thoughts like your Father thinks. Some of the people closest to you might talk about you behind your back or even abandon you, but don't let their actions discourage you or make you quit. Our Savior thought and lived very differently from most of those around Him—even the religious churchgoers of His day. He has not asked you to endure anything He Himself hasn't already gone through. More importantly, He promised to empower you by His Spirit to face anything that comes your way (see Philippians 4:13).

The best advice I can give you as we close this chapter is the timeless instruction given to us in Ephesians 4:23-24 AMPC:

> "...Be constantly renewed in the spirit of your mind [having a fresh mental and spiritual attitude], And put on the new nature (the regenerate self) created in God's image, [Godlike] in true righteousness and holiness."

As you renew your mind daily, your low thoughts will be replaced by higher thoughts, which will give way to higher actions. Before you know it, you will begin doing and accomplishing things by faith that others said couldn't be done. After everyone else counted you out, your life will rise again, but with more power and authority than ever before! God will get great glory through your life, and many who used to frustrate you will suddenly begin to imitate you because you had the courage to believe God and start thinking higher thoughts.

Chapter 12

WINNING THE WAR
FOR YOUR WORDS

*...If we could control our tongues, we would be perfect
and could also control ourselves in every other way.*
~James 3:2 (NLT)

"The potency of godly words can revive, heal, and
change our lives. Ungodly words have the power
to bind, imprison, and destroy."[36]

~Craig Groeschel

Words are unbelievably powerful. God Himself used His words to create life and all that we see in the world around us. He recorded the entire process for our benefit in Genesis 1-2. Every time God spoke, something new and productive was created. Light from darkness, land from water, vegetation from the earth, and on and on He spoke. When He was finished, He said everything He had created was *very good*.

You and I were created by God in His image, and we, too, possess the power of creation in our words. Unfortunately, not everything that we speak creates something good. Scripture is crystal clear:

"Death and life are in the power of the tongue, And those who love it will eat its fruit."

—Proverbs 18:21 (NASB)

As sure as there is a battle being fought for our thoughts, there is also a war being waged for our words. There is an inseparable connection between the thoughts we think and the words we speak. Every word formed on our tongue was first a thought solidified in our mind. Satan knows that if he can establish strongholds of low thinking in our minds, he can then dictate what comes out of our mouths. It is through our words that dynamic power is released—either life-giving or life-taking power.

Harnessing this power, which is right under our nose, is the focus of this final chapter. Together, we will explore the language of the liar—aka Satan—and how to avoid picking up his accent. We'll also identify five poisonous playlists we need to delete from our vocabulary. But first, let's begin by looking at some power principles from Scripture regarding our speech.

No Neutral Ground

One of the most important reasons for learning to think higher thoughts is to enable us to speak life-giving words. Apparently, when it comes to the power of our words, there is no such thing as *neutral*. Every time we open our mouths and speak, we are either giving life or taking it.

In a way, words are like money: they aren't necessarily good or evil. Their quality is determined by who they're coming from and how they're being used. Be it good or bad, we're constantly creating something with our words.

We can use our words to:

- Bless or curse
- Create friendships or make enemies
- Create reconciliation or incite division
- Create peace or pain

- Create an environment of encouragement or discouragement

Most marriages begin with the words "Will you marry me?" and sadly, many of them end with the words "I want a divorce." We can say "I love you" or "I hate you." We can say to someone, "Please forgive me," or we can spitefully shout, "You deserve what you got!" The choice is entirely up to us. So the question is not *if* we're creating something with our words, but rather *what are we creating?*

God has much to say about our words through the apostle James. Describing what the war for our words looks and sounds like, he says:

> "...No one can tame the tongue; it is a restless evil and full of deadly poison. With it we bless our Lord and Father, and with it we curse men, who have been made in the likeness of God; from the same mouth come both blessing and cursing. My brethren, these things ought not to be this way."

> **—James 3:8-10 (NASB)**

Can you see why there's such an intense war for your words? When the influence behind them falls into the wrong hands, that creative power suddenly becomes a dangerous weapon that results in death.

In his book *Soul Detox*, Pastor Craig Groeschel says that our words are...

> "Like a neutron bomb which annihilates human life but leaves buildings intact, words can devastate. Your body may remain unharmed, but your heart suffers the deadly shrapnel of painful phrases."[37]

Jesus also talked about the power that's in your words. In fact, in Matthew 12:36-37 (NLT), He offered a sobering warning:

"And I tell you this, you must give an account on judgment day for every idle word you speak. The words you say will either acquit you or condemn you."

Words carry great power—either releasing life or death. There is no such thing as neutral words. No one understands the implications of this reality better than your adversary the devil. **He knows that if he can hijack your *thought* life, he can hijack your *talk* life.** If successful, you become your own greatest enemy by placing in Satan's hands one of the most dangerous weapons in the world—your mouth. The most hurtful words you'll have to learn how to deal with are the ones that come out of your own mouth. That's why the first order of business is to clean up our bad language.

The Language of the Liar

Of the estimated 6,500 different languages spoken throughout the world, what is the most commonly spoken language? You may be surprised to discover that it's Mandarin, the official language of China, having over 1 billion speakers worldwide. The English language comes in a distant second with about 508 million speakers internationally.

Yet among the thousands of languages reported, there is one that has gone undetected. It's different from all the rest and is spoken on every continent, in every country, and has been heard by more people than the other 6,500 languages combined. No, you won't find this language listed in an encyclopedia because it's not a language of this world. It is a demonic dialect we hear every day but usually struggle to recognize. It is the language of deception. I call it the *language of the liar*.

Jesus described the dialect of the devil best when He said, "*...there is no truth in him. When he lies he speaks his native language, for he is a liar and the father of lies*" (John 8:44 NIV). In other words, if Satan tells you, "You could never become a great leader," it's because he knows that you can. If he says, "You could never make a difference with your life," it's because he's scared to death that you will. If he tells you, "It's too late in your life to become a good father, mother, husband, wife, or leader," it's because he doesn't want you to realize that you serve a God Who is the Author of time and is able to redeem whatever time you've lost. The truth is that as long as you're alive, God still has a plan for your life, and *nothing* is impossible with Him!

The longer you listen to the language of the liar, the less likely you will be to win the war for your words. The longer you allow the sound of his voice to invade your space, the easier it will become for you to start believing what he says is true. Eventually, you will start to "...exchange the truth of God for a lie" (see Romans 1:25).

Even worse, the longer you listen to the enemy, the more you will actually start to sound like him. That's what happened to the apostle Peter. At some point when he was serving in Jesus' ministry, Peter started listening to Satan's voice. This became evident from his response to Jesus right after He had finished sharing His plan of redemption with the disciples, which required Him to go to the cross. In a very unlikely manner, the Bible says:

> "Peter took Him aside and began to rebuke Him..."
>
> **—Matthew 16:22 (NIV)**

Have you ever stopped to think about what this verse says? It says that Peter *rebuked* the Lord. He rebuked THE Son of God, the all-knowing Creator of Heaven and earth! How in the world did Peter allow himself to step so far over this line? How did he allow those words to even come out of his mouth? The answer is discovered in Jesus' reply:

> "...Get behind Me, Satan! You are a stumbling block to Me; for you are not setting your mind on God's interests, but man's."
>
> **—Matthew 16:23 (NASB)**

Notice Jesus didn't say, "Get behind Me, *Peter!*" He said, "Get behind Me, *Satan!*" He addressed the voice behind the voice.

At some point Peter had stopped listening to the Life-Giver and started listening to the life-taker. Peter had become a victim of low thinking, and therefore had set his mind on man's interests rather than God's. He had been listening to the discouraging language of the liar for so long that he began to sound just like him. That's my point. Whatever voice we choose to spend time listening to is the voice we're going to sound like.

Do You Speak with an Accent?

You can usually tell who someone has been spending time with by the way they sound when they talk. For instance, maybe you have noticed that after you've spent time with people from a different part of the country (or the world for that matter), you might unknowingly start to pick up a little bit of their accent. If you're from the North like me, and you spend time in the South, before long you may unknowingly start to pick up a southern accent. This is actually a fairly common phenomenon that cognitive science refers to as *convergence*. This same principle holds true for us spiritually. Slowly, but surely, the more you listen to the language of the liar, the more you'll find yourself sounding and talking just like him.

At first it starts with indistinct changes in the tone of your attitude. Where you once used to be known for emphasizing the positive, you begin picking up a negative accent, and the emphasis of your words slowly, but steadily, begins leaning toward self-defeat. Initially, it is undetectable, except maybe to your spouse or close friends.

If you keep losing ground in the war for your words, the slightly bad accent will eventually turn into full-blown *bad language*. And no, I'm not necessarily talking about profanity. I'm talking about speaking the language of blame rather than blessing. I mean spending more time making excuses instead of making progress. More and more, you'll find yourself saying things like, "Nothing ever goes right for me. Things will never change." If the downward spiral continues, you'll begin replacing life-giving words with life-taking words:

- The words *I'm all in* will be replaced by *I quit.*
- *I can* will be exchanged for *I can't.*
- The words *I care* will be replaced by *Who cares?*
- *I forgive you* will be substituted by *I can't stand you!*

Satan and his demonic forces are highly skilled at using the people around us to speak some of the most deadly and damaging language into our lives, and he begins his assault when we are children. Teachers, coaches, spiritual leaders, and in some cases, even our parents became mouthpieces for the enemy. Think for a moment. Have you picked up unhealthy accents from your formative years?

- While you were growing up, did the people in your life speak the language of defeat?
- Did you pick up an accent of bitterness after you lost a job or went through a divorce?
- Do you go to work every day in a toxic environment where there's a heavy accent of negativity and pessimism that has started to rub off on you, and you don't know what to do to change your language back to one that reflects God's will for your life?

If any of these scenarios sound familiar, or you sense that somewhere in your life you're speaking the language of the liar, I've got great news for you! You don't have to keep speaking his demonic dialect. You can once again—or maybe for the very first time—learn how to speak the language of life! There are three basic steps required to deal with the deadly words and phrases you keep listening to in your mind and repeating with your mouth. They are:

1. *Identify* the poisonous playlists.
2. *Delete* the poisonous playlists.
3. *Replace* the poisonous playlists.

Identify the Poisonous Playlists

This first step is pretty straightforward. Recognize and pinpoint the specific negative, defeated, deadly words and phrases you hear in your mind and find yourself saying out loud. All that is necessary for you to do this is time and a willingness to be still and think about what you have been thinking about and talking about.

There's a powerful phrase in Psalm 46:10 (NKJV) that says, "Be still, and know that I am God..." If you will carve out about fifteen minutes a day to sit in God's presence and welcome His Spirit to help you identify the poisonous playlists, He will. Again, all you need is time and a willingness to be still and evaluate the ungodly thoughts and words you've been chewing and spewing. I'd encourage you to grab a notebook, draw a line down the center of the page, and write down on the left side the words and phrases you know need to be eradicated.

In Ephesians 4:29 (NASB), the apostle Paul wrote, "Let no unwholesome word proceed from your mouth, but only such a word as is good for edification..." We have a tendency to apply this principle to the way we talk to and about others, which is great. However, we also need to apply this truth to the way we talk to and about ourselves.

In order to learn which playlists need to be permanently deleted from your vocabulary, you'll have to be intentional about identifying your own bad language. This won't be easy at first, and yes, it's going to take some time to master. But if you're serious about thinking higher thoughts, and you invite God to help you, then you'll have what it takes to get your language under control by identifying all of the deadly words and phrases that tend to come out of your mouth.

Delete the Poisonous Playlists

Once you discover those recurring deadly words and phrases, you need to delete them from your vocabulary. More than anything, it's a daily decision. Choose to wake up every morning and make up your mind that you're going to win the war for your words. There is no need to rush this process, so be at peace. You have all the time you need to succeed as you keep with the pace of God's grace to experience change.

Replace the Poisonous Playlists

The third step I encourage you to take is to replace the wrong stuff with the right stuff. It won't be enough just to delete the bad. You'll also have to replace it with good. Jesus Himself taught us that eliminating the bad is a great start, but it's not enough. We also have to learn how to fill that empty space with something good.

If we neglect this step, it will only be a matter of time before bad language creeps back into the freshly vacated spaces in our vocabulary. Look at the principle Jesus gives us in Matthew 12:43-45 (NASB). He describes what happens when we evict a bad spirit and leave the space within us empty:

> "... When it comes, it finds [the space] unoccupied, swept, and put in order. Then it goes and takes along with it seven other spirits more wicked than itself, and they go in and live there; and the last state of that man becomes worse than the first..."

Now obviously in this example Jesus is specifically talking about demonic possession. Nevertheless, I believe the principle Jesus established here holds true for what we say and think. If you're going to win the war for your words and thoughts, then playing defense alone is not enough. You also have to learn how to play effective offense. That is, you need to develop some specific, life-giving words and phrases to counter and replace the old record that's been rolling off your lips. This is what you can use the right hand side of your notebook for. As you identify the deadly words and phrases you've been thinking and talking about, pray and search the Scriptures for life-giving replacements. I will give you an example of this in just a moment.

While specific negative words and phrases will vary from person to person, I want to spend the rest of our time together identifying *five poisonous playlists* in our vocabulary. These are things we've all either heard, have used ourselves, or have struggled with from time to time.

Poisonous Playlist #1
Negative Self-Talk

It's been said that we are able to speak about 500 words a minute out loud. Internally, however, we are able to speak an estimated 2,000 words to ourselves. If our *self-talk* is positive, healthy results will accompany it. If our self-talk is negative, unhealthy consequences are sure to follow. Look at this playlist of negative self-talk statements:

> *I'm so stupid! God, I look awful today. I'm such a slob. I never seem to do anything right. I'll never be a good leader. I'll never learn how to manage my money. I'll never be able to start my own business. I'm such a horrible writer; who would listen to anything I had to say, anyway? I'll never be healthy or in good physical shape. Who would ever want to marry me? I'll never be a good husband/wife/ mother/father. I'll never be organized or on time. I'll never change.*

This playlist could go on and on, but you get the idea. These examples of negative self-talk all pose a great threat to your life and must be dealt with.

In an article written by Dr. Susan Krauss for *Psychology Today*, Dr. Krauss actually reported that:

> "Researchers studying the thinking patterns of people with clinical levels of depression find that their self-talk tends toward a...relentless form of destructive self-talk."[38]

In other words, the more you hear yourself talk bad about yourself, the more you tend to believe what you've heard yourself say. The destructive cycle of negative self-talk sets in motion the worst kind of crippling synergy you can imagine. Your negative thoughts begin to feed your negative words, and then your negative words feed your negative thoughts. Before you know it you're sinking in an inescapable quicksand of negativity and defeat. If you don't break this vicious cycle, you won't just lose the war for your words, you may forfeit your very destiny. The bottom line is: stop repeating what the enemy whispers, and develop a new playlist!

The best way to delete the playlist of negative self-talk is to write down the areas in your life where you tend to put yourself down the most and the phrases you tend to say—internally and externally. These include comments like, *I hate my body. I'm so lazy. I don't have any talent. I'm not good at anything. I have the worst personality of anybody I know.*

Once you've written these down, start a new playlist by creating a second list right next to the first. For the new playlist, carefully pick positive, life-giving, vision-expanding words to replace the old statements of death and defeat. If speaking life doesn't come easy for you at first, just start by opening up your Bible. After all, the most life-giving words in the whole world are found in Scripture. Turn to the concordance in the back (if you have one—if not, search online), and look for key words that harmonize with the positive playlist you are trying to create. Your list might look something like this:

Life-Taking Playlist (To Be *Deleted*)	Life-Giving Playlist (To Be *Repeated*)
I hate the way I look.	I am fearfully and wonderfully made! (Ref: Psalm 139:14)
I'm not good at anything.	I am God's masterpiece—created to do good things that God planned for me long ago! (Ref: Ephesians 2:10)

Today's going to be a bad day.	This is the day that the Lord has made. I WILL rejoice and be glad in it! (Ref: Psalm 118:24)
I'll never be good with money.	"...for it is he Who gives you power to get wealth, that he may establish His covenant..." (Deuteronomy 8:18 AMPC)
I'm so stupid.	The Holy Spirit guides me into all truth. (Ref: John 16:13)

Every time you're tempted to speak from that poisonous playlist, check yourself, hit the delete button, and replace that old word or statement with your new one. If you've been stuck in a rut of negative self-talk for a long time, then speaking life over yourself is going to feel unnatural and awkward at first, but don't give up. If you stay committed, it will become a new way of life before you know it. The most exciting part is that just like speaking bad language is contagious, so is speaking life. It will begin to transform everything and everyone around you.

Poisonous Playlist #2
Chronic Complaining

This one is much like negative self-talk, except it's pointed outward rather than inward. Philippians 2:14 (NLT) tells us, "Do everything without complaining and arguing." Note the word *everything* in this verse. This indicates that complaining should never be the trademark of a Christian. If you've ever wondered how God feels about complaining, Numbers 11:1 offers us a pretty sobering glimpse on the matter.

"Soon the people began to *complain* about their hardship, and the Lord heard everything they said. Then the Lord's anger blazed against them..."

—Numbers 11:1 NLT

Complaining is contrary to the character of God. As a child of God created in His image, this should motivate you to work toward deleting this poisonous playlist from your vocabulary. Complaining also stifles your faith and keeps you from believing God, and without faith it is impossible to please God (see Hebrews 11:6).

Think for a minute. Have you ever personally been around someone who was a chronic complainer? Were they happy? How did you feel after you listened to them complain for a while? You probably felt drained and more than likely depressed when you walked away. That's because complaining takes life from you instead of giving life to you.

Complaining will discourage you to the point of saying, "Why should I even bother trying?" In fact, if you continue to complain, your spirit will start to feel depleted of faith and strength because every time you complain, it's like opening a drain in your soul and watching faith and hope spiral down like water from a bathtub.

The truth is, the areas of your life where you complain the most reveal the areas where you trust God the least. For instance, you can't say that you trust God with your money and then constantly complain about the economy. Likewise, you can't say that you trust God with your career and then constantly complain about your job. Actions like these are actually saying, "I trust You, God, BUT..."

The more we complain about how things look, the way people act, and the things people say that get on our nerves, the worse things begin to look. The reason is we're using our words to create a magnified picture of negativity in our lives. The way we view our spouse, our kids, our boss, our ministry leaders, our staff, etc., will greatly be reflected in the way we choose to talk about them.

The more negatively we talk, the more we program our minds to think negatively.

Clearly, complaining is the language of hopelessness. It's like praying in reverse. In fact, every time you complain, you miss a great opportunity to exercise your authority as a believer and speak life to your situation! The Bible teaches us that when we put our faith in Christ, He takes up residence in our own lives, and He gives us His authority to"...[call] those things which do not exist as though they did..." (Romans 4:17 NKJV). As people of faith, we have God-given authority in our voice, and we need to pay attention to how we use that authority.

Nothing will make God seem smaller and your problem look bigger than complaining. While complaining has the power to do nothing but make a bad situation worse, prayer packs the power to bring real change. Prayer and declaring the promises of God are perhaps the most powerful things you can do with your words.

If you're tired of the side effects of complaining, then it's time to delete and replace the playlist of chronic complaining from your life. Start by identifying and writing down the things you tend to complain about most. Then write some life-giving alternatives and begin to speak them. Or ask the people closest to you what areas of life they tend to hear you complain about the most. I can't promise you the negative situations around you are going to change just because you talk differently about them. However, I can promise you that the way you see them will. Like our Father, you'll begin to see things for what they could be rather than what they are now. So stop focusing on the things you can't control, and start focusing on what you can control—your words.

Poisonous Playlist #3
Gossiping

The third poisonous playlist that needs to be deleted is gossip—aka tale-bearing or slander. Let me be clear: There is no such thing as "good" gossip. All gossip is poisonous. It's hurtful, hateful, and serves only to divide and separate people. It is one of the most irresponsible things we can do with our words. As Eleanor Roosevelt said,

> "Great minds discuss ideas; average minds discuss events; small minds discuss people."[39]

Indeed, gossip is the language of the friendless and the insecure. It's the deadly dialect of the small-minded man or woman who has no regard for anyone other than themselves. The objective for the gossiper is always to make the object of his or her gossip look both weak and bad so that they (the gossiper) can feel powerful and good about themselves.

If you think about it, gossip is a verbal expression of lust—it's like having an affair verbally. Talking about others, especially those you are in relationship with, is like someone cheating on their marriage partner.

Like an adulterous affair...

- Gossip is a painful form of betrayal.
- Gossip is meant to be hidden from the people whom the gossiper is hurting.
- The gossiper usually pretends nothing is wrong when they're around the person they have gossiped about.
- The gossiper usually tries to justify their actions and paint their behavior as not really wrong.
- If you confront the gossiper, they will either deny they said anything or end the relationship.

As best as we can tell from Scripture, listening to gossip is not any better than speaking it. In fact, it will cost you dearly in the relational currency of integrity and credibility. God is so serious about the deadly nature of gossip that He gave us this warning in Leviticus 19:16 (NLT):

> "Do not spread slanderous gossip among your people. Do not stand idly by when your neighbor's life is threatened. I am the Lord."

As a recipient of gossip, you can be sure that at some point during the process of this verbal adultery, you'll be expected to not only agree with the gossiper but also reciprocate by sharing something equally juicy. If you don't, you'll run the risk of possibly becoming the next target of the gossiper's slander.

Proverbs 26:22 (NIV) says, "The words of a gossip are like choice morsels; they go down to the inmost parts." The juicy tidbits you hear may bring excitement initially, but if you keep listening to gossip, you'll eventually contract an STD—a Spiritually Transmitted Disease. That is, you yourself will become the one infected, spreading gossip to anyone and everyone who will listen.

The next time somebody starts to spread gossip about someone else, know that you have a responsibility to stand up and protect the other person's reputation. Simply walking away isn't enough. God wants you to speak up and not remain silent. When you hear gossip, address it on the spot. Don't wait until later to say something because the longer you wait to take action, the less likely you will be to do so. You don't have to be hateful or hurtful when you respond, but you do have to be truthful. You might simply say something like, "You know, this sounds and feels a lot like gossip to me. It makes me uncomfortable, and I'm not sure that anything good can come out of this conversation. Let's talk about something else."

Responding like this will not only protect the person being talked about, but also protect your integrity and credibility. It's unlikely that the person bringing you the gossip will bring it to you again. Now, some may ask, "But what if that person gets offended and doesn't talk to me anymore?" So be it. Probably the greatest gift a gossiper can give you is their absence.

Hopefully, it's becoming clear that gossip is destructive, demeaning, and according to the Bible, there's nothing that displeases God more. Through Solomon, the wisest man who ever lived, God said:

> "There are six things which the Lord hates, Yes, seven which are an abomination to Him: Haughty eyes, a lying tongue, And hands that shed innocent

blood, A heart that devises wicked plans, Feet that
run rapidly to evil, A false witness who utters lies,
And one who spreads strife among brothers."

—Proverbs 6:16-19 (NASB)

Did you notice in this proverb that the seventh thing—the
thing God calls an abomination—wasn't a lying tongue, haughty
eyes, or hands that shed innocent blood? The thing God hates
most is spreading gossip! It's the "...one who spreads strife among
brothers."

Friend, if you desire to think higher thoughts, the poisonous
playlist of gossip has got to go! If you have been gossiping, you
need to repent. You may need to go to those you've hurt with
your gossip and ask them for forgiveness too. I know that initially
this doesn't sound easy, but your purpose and potential are both
at stake. Please hear God's heart on this issue, and take it seriously. If you'll, "humble yourselves before the Lord...he will lift
you up in honor" (James 4:10 NLT).

Poisonous Playlist #4
Fear-Talk

The language of fear is another poisonous playlist you need
to be aware of and delete if it is operating in your life. Fear is the
antithesis of faith, and Scripture clearly states that "...God has not
given us a spirit of fear, but of power and of love and of a sound
mind" (2 Timothy 1:7 NKJV). Unfortunately, many believers are
giving voice to fear, and they're totally unaware. The reason for
this is that fear-talk usually masks itself with the guise of being a
"realist." Instead of taking risks, the realist chooses to stay in the
safety and comfort of what they're familiar with.

Let's face it: we live in a comfort-saturated culture, and we
will go to great lengths to obtain and protect our personal security. This includes making excuses to camouflage our real motiva-
tion for refusing to take a crucial step of faith God has prompted
us to make. When we fail to move forward, it leaves us and those

the Lord has called us to help on the losing end. In the eloquent words my wife has uttered so often, "Our blessings are often tied up in the things that *we won't* do for God."

Whenever God calls us to take a step of faith, we'll be tempted to start speaking the language of fear. If we give in to the temptation, we'll frequently find ourselves citing all of the reasons why a new idea will never work. We'll constantly be talking about what could and "probably will" go wrong. In an effort to remain concealed and avoid being confronted, the spirit of fear will then offer us excuses, using phrases like:

- "What if…"
- "What about the money…?"
- "Well, you never know what could happen…"
- "I'd rather be safe than sorry." (I'm so glad Jesus didn't decide to play it safe!)
- "It's just not the right time."
- "If it's meant to be, it's meant to be."

Most of the time when we make excuses, it's to avoid the *question marks* in our lives—that is, the unknown zone that stands between where we are and where God has called us to go. It's the question marks that the spirit of fear keeps pointing to whenever we are about to take a crucial step of faith. Rather than face our fears, we often succumb to the temptation to excuse ourselves from fear's presence. However, when we do, we also unknowingly excuse ourselves from the pursuit of our purpose.

"But aren't we supposed to follow peace?" you may ask, and the answer is yes and no. Let me explain. Yes, you are to follow the peace of God that He gives you in your *spirit*. But having peace in your emotions is highly unlikely. When you're making a major decision in life, your natural feelings are going to be afraid. However, if God is calling you to step out and do something, He will give you an inner peace even while your natural emotions are freaking out. If you go through life with the goal of always having peace in your emotions, you may be comfortable, but you'll never experience the miraculous. Your life will be limited to only reading the stories and listening to the testimonies of other people's faith.

As you can see, fear-talk isn't always as obvious as we think it is, and because words are like seeds, fear-talk will not only affect you, but also the people around you. The more you allow yourself to speak with the language of fear, the more your spouse, kids, and others will begin to pick up your bad accent.

There's only one way to kill fear. Confront it by faith. Walk right up to it, look it in the eye, and then smile as you walk past it! Fear will always attempt to stand between you and your purpose, but you don't have to cower and run away. You can pray and draw strength from God's Spirit to stand against it and keep walking.

Remember, when you start deleting a poisonous playlist from your vocabulary, you'll need to replace the negative with the positive. In this case, replace excuses and words of fear with words of faith. Rather than citing all the things that could go wrong, start declaring the truth: "If God be for me, than who can stand against me?" (See Romans 8:31.) "I am more than a conqueror through Christ!" (See Romans 8:37.) And, "I can do all things through Christ who gives me strength." (See Philippians 4:13.) Take time regularly to remind yourself of all the times God has come through for you, and no matter how things look right now, God is still your provider!

Poisonous Playlist #5
Holding onto the Past

With this fifth poisonous playlist, I'll be brief and to the point. Ready? Here it is: You cannot move forward as long as you keep looking backward. Constantly bringing up the past will never move you into your future. Whether it's your past or someone else's past that's affected you, you have to let it go. This is especially true for us who have a personal relationship with Jesus. Second Corinthians 5:17 (NASB) declares:

> "...If anyone is in Christ, he is a new creature;
> the old things passed away; behold, new things
> have come."

Are there past sins you've asked God to forgive you of, but you're still holding onto? If so, what right do you have to hold onto what God has forgiven? Let it go! Stop talking about it! Constantly verbalizing your past failures will keep you from moving forward and fulfilling your God-ordained purpose. Whether it was something you did to yourself or something someone else did to you, every time you speak about it, you give it new life. The past is one thing you need to suffocate by refusing to give it CPR which is what happens every time you bring it back up. In fact, the best way to handle your past is to follow the advice the apostle Paul gave in Philippians 3:13-14 (NASB):

> "...But one thing I do: forgetting what lies behind
> and reaching forward to what lies ahead, I press
> on toward the goal for the prize of the upward call
> of God in Christ Jesus."

You can't start thinking about what's ahead of you until you first stop talking about what's behind you. The past is called the past because it has passed. The way to delete this poisonous playlist from your vocabulary is by using the F-word: *Forgive!* Forgive yourself, forgive your family, forgive your friends, and forgive anyone who's hurt you. When you forgive, you release yourself from the prison of the past and position yourself for your future ahead. When bad feelings rise up and try to pull you back into bondage, begin to pray blessings on those who hurt you. God has great things ahead, and you will experience them as you choose to leave the past in the past.

(Please refer back to Chapter 9 for the steps to walking in forgiveness.)

Dead Silence

There's one last playlist I want to mention before we conclude, and it may be the most overlooked playlist of all. I call it *The Empty Playlist*—aka *dead silence.* It's everything that you should be saying but don't. It's holding back words of life when you have it in your power to give them. This is like denying the people in your life the emotional and spiritual oxygen they need to live. It's not enough to not say bad things. We have a divine responsibility to learn how to say good things. Let me illustrate with this example.

Imagine a highly skilled paramedic sitting in a restaurant booth downtown eating lunch. Suddenly, about fifteen feet from where he is seated, he notices a young elementary-aged girl beginning to choke violently. As a paramedic he possesses years of experience and training in saving people's lives. He has both the tools and the ability to rescue the little girl from death, yet he remains seated. Onlookers at neighboring tables begin to panic because the little girl's face is now purple as she struggles to catch her next breath. Still the paramedic does nothing but watch from a distance. Despite the torrential tears pouring from the eyes of the child's mother and the look of sheer terror now gripping the little girl's face, the paramedic continues to sit and eat his meal unmoved. He simply doesn't want to be bothered.

In a similar way, there are people all around us every day who are mentally, emotionally, and spiritually struggling to survive. They are choking on their feelings of fear, insecurity, depression, or inferiority. God has given us the power to speak life into them and save their lives. Unfortunately, like the paramedic in our parable, we often sit in silence and watch from a distance, choosing to do nothing / say nothing. In those moments, we are just as guilty as that paramedic. That's why I call this section "Dead Silence," because our choice not to speak can actually result in physical, relational, and emotional death. Marriages have ended because of dead silence. Churches have deteriorated because of dead silence. Relationships between parents and children that could have been saved if someone would have just opened their mouths and spoken life have died because of dead silence.

The Word of God is clear: "Death and life are in the power of the tongue..." (Proverbs 18:21 NASB), and we have a responsibility to use that power to speak words of life to those in need. Again and again, we are directed by God to take action and do good when we have the opportunity.

Scripture says:

> "Do not withhold good from those who deserve it when it's in your power to help them."

—Proverbs 3:27 (NLT)

> "...As we have opportunity, let us do good to all people, especially to those who belong to the family of believers."

—Galatians 6:10 (NIV)

Friend, don't withhold life-giving words from the people around you when it's in your power to help them. Remember that "Anxiety in a man's heart weighs it down, But a good word makes it glad" (Proverbs 12:25 NASB). You can transform someone's life by simply paying them a compliment or speaking to the God-given potential within.

Don't assume your husband or wife knows how much you appreciate what they do for you and your family. Go out of your way to tell them they are doing a great job, and be specific! Nothing feels more disingenuous than a generic compliment. Don't just say, "You're doing a good job." Take it a step further and tell them what they're doing that you really appreciate and admire. Build up your spouse, your kids, your coworkers, and your friends by speaking life-giving words of praise.

I also encourage you to affirm them in the things that they love to do instead of just nagging them for all of the things you don't think they do well. Again, never assume that your children or spouse knows how proud you are of them. Tell them. Learn how to take an interest in other people's lives and speak words of encouragement. You have the power to literally change somebody's life if you'll just choose to use your words!

Win the War for Your Words!

As we wrap up this chapter, I challenge you to refuse to listen to the language of the liar and start spending more time saturating yourself in the Word of God, prayer, and other life-giving resources. As you do, you will turn the tide of this war for your words and begin cultivating a Kingdom accent.

When you're tempted to speak negatively, and you hear those old poisonous playlists trying to creep back into your vocabulary, choose to press eject and replace them with life-giving alternatives, including thanksgiving and worship. Pray as the psalmist David prayed: "Set a guard, O Lord, over my mouth; Keep watch over the door of my lips" (Psalm 141:3 NASB).

When you're tempted to get pulled into a gossip session at work, at church, or with a family member, lovingly let them know that you'll have no part in it. If they keep talking, walk away. Refuse to allow those negative seeds to be planted in your mind. The apostle Paul tells us in 1 Corinthians 15:33 (NIV) that "...Bad company corrupts good character." So if you're surrounded by people who are always speaking negative and destructive language, then you may need to reevaluate your relationships—or at the very least, draw some boundaries around the kind of conversations you'll allow yourself to have with them.

In the end, the principle of spiritual convergence holds true for the positive just as it does for the negative. In other words, just like listening to the language of the life-taker can rub off on us, so can listening to the language of the Life-Giver! The best way to start cultivating a Kingdom accent is to simply start spending more time with the King and the people of His Kingdom. This is one of the reasons why being a part of a vibrant church is so important. The more time you spend in the Father's house with life-speaking brothers and sisters in Christ, the more you'll pick up the accent of your Father. I believe that's one of the main reasons Hebrews 10:25 (NASB) tells us not to forsake "...our own assembling together, as is the habit of some, but encouraging one another..." as we come together.

You might not be able to do anything about your past or the language of the people around you, but you certainly can do something about you. It's time to begin developing a dialect God desires. So thank Him for what you do have. Thank Him for His love and His divine favor on your life. Thank Him for helping you use your words to breathe life into those around you. Ask God to help you recognize and defeat these seven deadly thoughts, and before you know it, you'll be well on your way to winning the war for your words!

ENDNOTES

Chapter 1

1 "Quotable Quote," Goodreads (accessed June 1, 2018), https://www.goodreads.com/quotes/33921-change-your-thoughts-and-you-change-your-world.

2 Joyce Meyer, *Battlefield of the Mind Devotional: 100 Insights That Will Change the Way You Think* (New York: FaithWords, 2005), 8.

Chapter 2

3 "Quotable Quote," Goodreads (accessed January 14, 2018), https://www.goodreads.com/quotes/87185-progress-is-im-possible-without-change-and-those-who-cannot-change.

4 Joel Osteen, *Your Best Life Now: 7 Steps to Living at Your Full Potential* (New York: FaithWords, 2014), 72-73.

5 Mark Banschick, "The High Failure Rate of Second and Third Marriages," *Psychology Today* (February 6, 2012), https://www.psychology-today.com/us/blog/the-intelligent-divorce/201202/the-high-failure-rate-second-and-third-marriages.

6 Maxwell, John. *Attitude 101: What Every Leader Needs to Know.* Thomas Nelson. Kindle Edition.

7 John C. Maxwell, *Attitude 101: What Every Leader Needs to Know* (Nashville: Thomas Nelson, 2003), 31-32.

8   Craig Groeschel, *Altar Ego: Becoming Who God Says You Are* (Grand Rapids: Zondervan, 2013), 55.

Chapter 3
9   "Lead Poisoning", Mayo Clinic, accessed March 16, 2019, https://www.mayoclinic.org/diseases-conditions/lead-poisoning/symptoms-causes/syc-20354717.

Chapter 4
10 "Quotable Quote," Goodreads (accessed May 11, 2019), https://www.goodreads.com/quotes/21546-our-doubts-are-traitors-and-make-us-lose-the-good.

Chapter 5
11 Chand, Samuel R. New Thinking, New Future (p. 60). Whitaker House. Kindle Edition.

12 Peter Scazzero, *The Emotionally Healthy Leader: How Transforming Your Inner Life Will Deeply Transform Your Church, Team, and the World* (Grand Rapids: Zondervan, 2015), 55.

Chapter 6
13 Gary L. Thomas, *Thirsting for God: Spiritual Refreshment for the Sacred Journey* (Eugene: Harvest House Publishers, 2011), 137.

14 Pringle, Phil. Top 10 Qualities of a Great Leader (p. 99). Harrison House LLC. Kindle Edition.

15 Thomas, Gary L. Thirsting for God (Kindle Locations 2411-2413). Harvest House Publishers. Kindle Edition.

16 Thomas, Gary

17 Thomas, Gary

18 Murray, Andrew, Humility (Kindle Edition: Whitaker House, 1982).

19 Murray, Andrew, Humility.

Chapter 7

20 "Franklin D. Roosevelt Quotes," BrainyQuote (accessed December 14, 2020),

21 Mark Batterson, *The Grave Robber: How Jesus Can Make Your Impossible Possible* (Grand Rapids: Baker Books, 2014), 104.

Chapter 8

22 T.D. Jakes, "T.D. Jakes Sermons: It's Not What It Looks Like," YouTube (December 26, 2014), https://www.youtube.com/watch?v=JVOZ7DEfolc.

Chapter 9

23 "Quotable Quote," Goodreads (accessed August 22, 2019), https://www.goodreads.com/quotes/843513-when-you-forgive-you-in-no-way-change-the-past.

24 "John Burroughs Quotes," BrainyQuote (accessed September 8, 2018), https://www.brainyquote.com/quotes/john_burroughs_150288.

25 Brad Krause, "Cancer Patients Embrace Forgiveness Therapy and Other Self-Care Strategies," (July 9, 2018), https://internationalforgiveness.wordpress.com/2018/07/09/cancer-patients-embrace-forgiveness-therapy-and-other-self-care-strategies.

26 Swartz, Karen. "Forgiveness: Your Health Depends on It." *Johns Hopkins Medicine*, 2020, 3:47pm, www.hopkinsmedicine.org/health/wellness-and-prevention/forgiveness-your-health-depends-on-it.

Chapter 10

27 "Why You Should Embrace Discomfort", Michaelhyatt.com, accessed December 22, 2020, https://michaelhyatt.com/why-discomfort-is-good-for-you/

28 Samuel R. Chand, Leadership Pain: The Classroom for Growth (Nashville: Thomas Nelson, 2015), 157.

29 Bishop Dale C. Bronner, Senior Pastor Word of Faith Family Worship Cathedral.

Chapter 11

30 "Franklin D. Roosevelt Quotes," BrainyQuote (accessed July 9, 2019), https://www.brainyquote.com/quotes/franklin_d_roosevelt_130048.

31 Joyce Meyer, *Battlefield of the Mind: Winning the Battle in Your Mind* (New York: Warner Books, 1995), 15.

32 T.D. Jakes, *Instinct: The Power to Unleash Your Inborn Drive* (New York: FaithWords, 2014), 128.

33 TEDx Talks, "Draw your future | Patti Dobrowolski | TEDxRainier," YouTube (June 10, 2012), https://www.youtube.com/watch?v=zESeeaFDVSw.

34 Ron Carpenter, Jr., "Relationship Builder Blog."

35 Ron Carpenter, Jr., *The Necessity of an Enemy: How the Battle You Face Is Your Best Opportunity* (Colorado Springs: WaterBrook Press, 2012), 122.

Chapter 12

36 Craig Groeschel, *Soul Detox: Clean Living in a Contaminated World* (Grand Rapids: Zondervan, 2012), 57.

37 Groeschel, *Soul Detox*, 56.

38 Susan Krauss Whitbourne, "Make Your Self-Talk Work for You," *Psychology Today* (September 10, 2013), https://www.psychologytoday.com/us/blog/fulfillment-any-age/201309/make-your-self-talk-work-you.

39 "Great Minds Discuss Ideas; Average Minds Discuss Events; Small Minds Discuss People," Quote Investigator

(accessed October 14, 2019), https://quoteinvestigator.com/2014/11/18/great-minds.

Made in the USA
Columbia, SC
20 June 2021